Foreword

Young Writers was established in 1991 and has been passionately devoted to the promotion of reading and writing in children and young adults ever since. The quest continues today. Young Writers remains as committed to engendering the fostering of burgeoning poetic and literary talent as ever.

This year's Young Writers competition has proven as vibrant and dynamic as ever and we are delighted to present a showcase of the best poetry from across the UK. Each poem has been carefully selected from a wealth of *Once Upon A Rhyme* entries before ultimately being published in this, our twelfth primary school poetry series.

Once again, we have been supremely impressed by the overall high quality of the entries we have received. The imagination, energy and creativity which has gone into each young writer's entry made choosing the best poems a challenging and often difficult but ultimately hugely rewarding task - the general high standard of the work submitted amply vindicating this opportunity to bring their poetry to a larger appreciative audience.

We sincerely hope you are pleased with our final selection and that you will enjoy *Once Upon A Rhyme Fife* for many years to come.

Young Writers

2004 POETRY COMPETITION

ONCE UPON A RHYME

IMAGINATION FOR A NEW GENERATION

Fife

Edited by Steve Twelvetree

 Young**Writers**

First published in Great Britain in 2004 by:
Young Writers
Remus House
Coltsfoot Drive
Peterborough
PE2 9JX
Telephone: 01733 890066
Website: www.youngwriters.co.uk

SB ISBN 1 84460 466 7

Contents

Emma Johnstone (10)   17
Rebecca Wilson (10)   18
Hannah O'Connor (10)   19
Lyndsay Graham (10)   19
Julie-Anne Mullady (10)   20
Amy Judge (10)   20
Andrew Gibson (10)   21

Cleish Primary School
Andrew Forbes (8)   21
Ruaridh Stevenson (8)   21
Lewis Hunter (9)   22
Stuart Hunter (11)   22
Adam Cunningham (9)   23
Catriona Blair (10)   23

Crail Primary School
Ryan Petrie (8)   24
Michelle Murray (8)   24
Laura Wilson (8)   24
Sean Barnes (8)   25
Rebecca Grieve (10)   25
Blair Watson (8)   25
Alice Rhodes (10)   26
Chloe Forsyth (10)   26
Bryony Harper (10)   27
Katie Wilson (10)   27
Nicole Petrie (10)   27
Kirsten McKay (10)   28
Kelvin Budd (11)   28
Joanne Stockwell (10)   28
Emily Paterson (11)   29
James Stewart (11)   29
Lucy Chalmers (8)   29
Claire Thomson (8)   30
Katie Clayton (11)   30

Creich Primary School
Fiona Cuthill (10)   31
Hayley Rees (11)   32

Mhairi Roberts (8) & Hannah Fricke (7)   33
James Barker (11)   34
Craig Roberts (11)   35

Dunbog Primary School
Euan Stewart (11)   35
Donald Stewart (11)   36
Christian Smith (10)   36
Robert Struthers (10)   37
Chloe Gordon (7)   37
Ben Kerridge (11)   38

Dysart Primary School
Sean Sirur (7)   38
Gary Paterson (7)   39
Brian Smith (7)   39
Rory Smith (7)   40
Aarron Balfour (11)   40
Ross Leslie (10)   41
Christina Sinclair (10)   41
Natalie Galloway (11)   42
Gaby Leslie (8)   42
Toni Walton (11)   43
Emma Wilson (10)   43
Joshua Wilkinson (10)   44
Kerry Lister (11)   44
Keighley Paterson (10)   45
Danielle Cunningham (10)   45
Gemma Morrison (10)   46
Darrel Johnston (10)   46
Kayleigh Bannerman (10)   47
Alex Mill (7)   47
Dylan Anderson (7)   48

Greyfriars RC Primary School
Lucy Nash (9)   48
Oliver Grieve (8)   49
Courtney Thom (8)   49
Dily Mordi (8)   50
Jonathan Watson (8)   50

Harvey Leicester (8)	51
Andro Mathewson (8)	51
Francesca Baldacchino (9)	52
Lewis Rae (9)	52
Dougal MacEwan (8)	53
Connor Morrison	53
Oliver Cocris (8)	54
Michal Martin (9)	54
Sadie Irving (8)	55
Bridie Lamb (8)	55
Jasmine King (8)	56
Emily Christianson (8)	56
Natalie Northridge (8)	57
Courtney Gatherum (8)	57

Inverkeithing Primary School

Kirsten McBride	57
Simon Thomas (10)	58
Chanise Harvey (10)	58
Aileen Simpson (10)	58
Jessica Barrie (10)	59
Ryan Williams (9)	59
Greg Milne (10)	59
Emma Black (10)	60
Craig Melvin (10)	60
Carmel Wilkinson-Ayre (10)	60
Laura Watts (11)	61
Rachael Barrie (11)	62
Aimee Minty (11)	62
Jordan Sadler (10)	63
Catherine Ostrom (9)	63
Holly Paterson (9)	64
Natasha Briggs (9)	64
Fiona Hunter (9)	65
Daniel Horn & Aidan Smith (9)	65
Hannah Masterton (7)	65
Adam Parsley (7)	66
Gavin Simpson (7)	66
Taylor Galloway (7)	66
Christopher Ostrom (7)	67
Lesley Anne Reid (10)	67

Mark Cannon (10)   67
Daniel Cameron (10)   68
Kyle Wright (10)   68

Kennoway Primary & Community School
David Wellsted (8)   68
Jennifer Rankin (10)   69
Dominic Curran (7)   69
Abbie Staig (7)   70
Hollie Ford (10)   70
Megan Pullar (10)   71
Tanya Charles (7)   71
Craig Docherty (10)   72
Sam Docherty (7)   72
Callum Hynd (7)   73
Ian Fraser (11)   73
Blair Johnstone (10)   74
Joshua Smith (10)   75
Craig Donnelly (10)   76
Thomas Fraser (11)   77
Megan Penny (11)   77
Nicole Fortune (11)   78
Casey Galloway (11)   78
Louise Gilmour (11)   79
Aaron Wilson (11)   79
Ashley Farmer (11)   80

Kinglassie Primary School
Adam Terris (11)   80
Melanie Burns (11)   81
Abbie Hutchison (11)   81
Danielle Gaughan (11)   82
Chloe Taylor (10)   82
Gemma Fleming (11)   82
John Naylor (11)   83

Ladybank Primary School
Ashleigh Thomson (11)   83
Catriona Duncan (11)   84
Ceri Griffiths (11)   84

Andrew Anderson (10)   85
Callum Murray (11)   85
Jack Wright (11)   86
Russell Hope (11)   86
Amy Chalmers (11)   87
Victoria Robertson (11)   87
Annabel Laura Baker (11)   88
Luke Crawford (11)   88
Lindsay McDiarmid (11)   89

Lochgelly South Primary School
Megan Dick (9)   90
Megan Waterson (9)   90
Lauren Adams (9)   91
Lewis Hamill (9)   91
Shannen Hunter (9)   92
Amy Fong (9)   92
Amy Kearns (9)   93
Kirsty Young (9)   93
James Bernard (9)   94
Kyle Brockie (9)   95

Lynburn Primary School
Becci Douglass (11)   95
Jade Kehoe (11)   96
Ewan Paterson (11)   97
Stuart Taylor (11)   98
Craig Forbes (11)   99
Sarah-Jane Dale (11)   100
David J McManus (11)   101
Darryl Simpson (11)   102
Michael Wilson (11)   103
Samantha Fraser (11)   104
Clare Gourlay (11)   105
Erin McRae (11)   105
Sam Gibson (11)   106
Kirsty Muir (11)   106
Gemma Day (11)   107
Leaha Robertson (11)   107
Cheryl Cowan (11)   108
Neal Mullen (11)   109

Newburgh Primary School

Pitcoudie Primary School

St Leonards Middle School, St Andrews

Jasmine Wilson (9)	162
Mary Ann McKechnie (10)	162
Hannah Gray (8)	163
Joanna MacKay (10)	163
Robert Clark (9)	164
Josh Jamieson (10)	164
Cameron Spencer (9)	165
Charlotte Lorimer (8)	165
Danny Stewart (8)	166
Zak Maas (10)	166
Olivia Gibson (8)	167
Richard Ward (9)	167
Natalie De Groot (9)	168
Nina Duncan (8)	168
Alice Ferguson (10)	169
Alexander Murray (10)	170
Ged Rutherford (9)	170
Flora Ogilvy (9)	171
Izak Maas (9)	172
Sara Aguilar (10)	172
Liam Deboys (11)	173
Holly Milne (8)	173
Jamie Morse (8)	174
Victoria Baillie (10)	174
Charlotte Lindesay-Bethune (10)	175
Iain Watson (10)	176
Louise Cox (10)	177
Annabel Zajicek (9)	177
Amber Wilson (10)	178
Emily Allen (10)	179
Lily Ratcliff (8)	179
Cassia Littler (10)	180
Keir Hunter (8)	181
Fraser Gillan (8)	181
Angus Littleford (8)	182
Katie Overend (8)	182

St Monans Primary School, St Monans

Liam Tarvit (10)	183
Megan Gilbert (10)	183

Lindzi Tarvit (10)	184
Rachael Clarke (10)	184
Douglas Hughes (9)	185
Tyler King (10)	185
Jordan McMullan (10)	185
Graeme Guthrie	186
Kiyrie McLellan (9)	186
Ryan Leitch (9)	187
Jamie Allen (10)	187

St Ninian's Primary School, Cardenden

Stefan Fraser (11)	188
Michael Donaldson (11)	188
Christopher Inglis (11)	189
Sarah-Louise Mckie (11)	189
John Kay (11)	190
Nicole Curran (11)	190

Tayport Primary School

Owen Stewart (10)	190
Danny Arnold (10)	191
Kayleigh Paterson (11)	191
Sophie Brown (11)	192
Jennifer Brown (11)	192
Ross Noble (11)	193
Craig Bell (11)	193
Steven Lough (12)	194
Ben Parihar (10)	194
Amy Jones (11)	195
Jade McRitchie (10)	195
Louisa Reid (10)	196
Alice Minick (11)	196
Erica Lowe (10)	197
Dale Brownless (11)	197
Nell Glen (11)	198
Johanna Beat (11)	199
Koren Anderson (11)	199
Michael Greig (11)	200
Catherine Carson (11)	200
Charlotte Hanlon (11)	201
Hayley Leitch (11)	201

The Poems

Summer

S ounds of glee fill the air
U nder the sea, clear blue
M y dad making burgers and
M y mum making us laugh
E veryone relaxed except me
R unning around after my cousins!

Natalie Winton (11)
Capshard Primary School

Sam Nixon

I have an idol,
I'm sure he will be for years.
He was a smile to wipe away tears
I can't explain the blast of excitement
At the mention of his name.
　　Sam Nixon is my idol.

My room is drowning in posters of him,
He is my hero, he will always be.
Hair like a razor, can't you see.
A voice so heavenly.
　　Sam Nixon is my idol.

Claire Wheelan (11)
Capshard Primary School

Hunting

H urrying along, foxes run from the black hunter,
U nable to see his face, you can only see his
N oble stallion with fiery red eyes,
T ime and time again he uses his black gun,
I n fright foxes hide in bushes but are found.
N owhere to hide, they howl for help. The
G un fires balls of light until every last fox is dead.

Caroline B Smith (11)
Capshard Primary School

Netball

N etball, I play it after school
E veryone enjoying
T he excitement as the
B all bounces high
A nd out of our reach
L ow and high
L ike a bird soaring.

Linzi Smart (11)
Capshard Primary School

Night-Time

N ight-time falls and all
I s still. People
G et ready for bed.
H ear the babies wail as they get
T ucked in.

T hough everybody's fast asleep
I n the sheet of darkness,
M any nocturnal animals stir.
E vening has gone . . . to be replaced by night.

Kathryn Sim (11)
Capshard Primary School

Snow

S mooth brushing dust, angels in the snow
N ever going away. Fluffy, smooth and fine
O n the window ledge silky and slushy
W hite winter snow.

Darren Robertson (11)
Capshard Primary School

Dear Diary

Dear Diary,
I am worried, I think I know why
I am getting bullied
I'm living a lie
I told the girl that I do not care
But I do, I do, she pulls my hair.

Dear Diary,
Today you won't guess,
It happened again
My life's a mess.

Dear Diary,
Everyday that I go out
She's always there
And out and about
Her brutal face, it's there as well
Shouting at me like a furious bell.

Dear Diary,
It's the conclusion, it's the end,
I don't want to be bullied
Not again.

Christina Robertson (11)
Capshard Primary School

Summer

S ummer in our house is always great
U nder the tree my dad is on the barbecue
M aking yummy hamburgers
M y rabbit's lying down in the sun
E veryone loves summer
R unning about having a water fight.

Emma Reid (11)
Capshard Primary School

Snow And Ice

Snow - a white, silk sheet,
Falling from the sky.
Soft and light, not heavy.
Lost in a white, wonderful land
I see nothing but the big snowflakes falling.

Icicles, like sharp pointed knives
Hanging from the roof.
Sleek and soft to touch.
When you look in them they are like mirrors,
Clear to see through.
Like glass windows just cleaned.

Rachael Reid (11)
Capshard Primary School

Ice Hockey

Ice hockey, my favourite sport
I love playing it.
Throwing hard hits
Great feeling as you step on the white blanket.

Great when you score!
You've opened the door.
Skating in shoals
Setting up goals.

Winning trophies with all your might.
Your parents
Are sure to be
Full of delight.

With breakaways you're under pressure
As you skate on
The white blanket
Ruffles appear.

Michael Greig (11)
Capshard Primary School

Tia

Tia is as furry as a fur ball
When she shakes her fur
She turns to a teddy.
When Tia is upset or wants something
She puts her sweet adorable little puppy eyes on.

When you shout, Tia stares at you
With her cute little squashed face
And when she knows
That she has done something wrong
She puts an innocent face on.

Lovely golden blonde hair
Dark brown eyes
And a curly tail like a pig.
What a moany dog! When she barks
She'll drive you up the wall.

I'm so glad to have a dog like Tia!

Gemma Ketchen (11)
Capshard Primary School

Basketball

B asketball is the best sport
A ll the time the ball in the hoop the
S uper LA Lakers
K ings of basketball
E veryone's a winner
T ime passes by easily. The
B all is great
A t throwing in the
L A
L aker's hoop. They score!

Ryan Lafferty (11)
Capshard Primary School

Snuffles

Snuffles! Snuffles as white as snow
his half moustache, makes me so joyful
and his tail is small and white
Snuffles! Snuffles his big, long, black line matching his coat.

Snuffles! Snuffles all of his whiskers are white
except one is black and a brown birthmark on his lip.
Wouldn't take another pet.
Snuffles!

Blair Nixon (10)
Capshard Primary School

Football

F ootie is great
O h! he just about scored
O h! he hit the post
T he opponent team scores
B ad for us
A nd good for them
L osing at half-time but then it all changed
L aughing and cheering as we make our way home.

Scott Nisbet (11)
Capshard Primary School

Candy

C aramel coloured fur
A nd a white tickly tummy
N ibbling at her treats
D igging day and night
Y ou'll always want to hold her.

Natalie Mearns (11)
Capshard Primary School

Football

F ootball! The best game
O f history strikers dodging
O ut and in
T hrough
B ig bold defenders
A ttacking with pace
L aunching into tackles
L eaving a path behind them.

Grant McGowan (11)
Capshard Primary School

Rabbit

R abbits! Cute, snuggly and warm
A black and
B rownie-orange - that's mine! When he runs across
   the hard floor he is like a mouse.
B abies, when they fall asleep are like him
I n my arms, snuggling in
T iny Bambi, baby deer jumping about in the wild.

Ashleigh Bell (11)
Capshard Primary School

Skateboarding

The roaring of wheels
Moving along swiftly across the path.
The man, like a giant nightlight
For the world to see.
The path begins to look like space
With its padded blanket.
Skateboarding is something to stay with.

Lee Haxton (11)
Capshard Primary School

Snow

Cosy inside me.
The snow falling outside my window
Like a lace curtain.
When I'm outside touching snow
It feels like
Soft, white polar bear skin.

Children wrapped up, building snowmen,
Whoosh! There goes a snowball,
All the kids laughing, making snow angels.

Snowmen melt, icicles drop.
In go the red rosy cheeked children
To snuggle by the fire!

Stephanie Milne (11)
Capshard Primary School

Summertime

S ummertime, sun shining bright.
U mbrellas don't go up.
M ornings get brighter day by day.
M any families away on picnics.
E very animal waking from hibernation.
R igid and tall stand the trees,
T heir leaves back upon the branches.
I smell freshly cut grass
M agically coloured flowers!
E very one beautifully perfumed.

Heather Ferrier (11)
Capshard Primary School

Betrayal

Cutting blades of the death carriage killing all the clouds,
Inside we are carried which our deaths are decided.
The green and black camouflage making it stick out in the clouds,
Not hiding it from the things in the sky who all avoid us.

I worry about my squad; they don't know what is coming.
We are all guns for hire but not for this type of thing.
It's all just a cover-up, a cover-up for me, me and a couple
Of other people who must survive to be free.

More death carriages appear in the gloom of the night.
People's faces in glassed windows, men and women alike.
They look so pale like the ghosts they might become.
Platoon A, B, C and D are all going to die. This is our fate.

I see the clouds vanishing as we descend to the ground,
The city coming into sight, burning in the darkness.
Distant cries of unknown creatures, killing everything that moves.
These creatures are our doom. God save us all.

Air waves waving as the wheels touch the ground.
The smell of rotting flesh in the air. Unhuman screams
Should I put my watch dog duty first and let my men die?
Never! I will not put my job first. I will not betray my squad.

Kenneth Baird (11)
Capshard Primary School

Swimming

S wimming in the pool
W hizzing up and down
 I feel like a fish in the sea
M y feet are kicking hard and
M y arms turning fast
 I n a clockwise direction. I see
N othing but splashing in the air
G old! I won the race.

Claire Buist (11)
Capshard Primary School

Summer

Children coming out to play
Winter's gone . . . hooray!
The incredible heat on the pavement below my feet
Sun is blazing on the street
In the sky not a single cloud
Fun and laughter all around
It's the time of year when the sun's about
Summer . . .
The best season to be out!

Claire Borthwick (11)
Capshard Primary School

Why Do I Try?

Why do I try to fit in
  when my life ends up in the bin?
   Oh why can't I drink a bottle of gin?

    I always try my best
     I'm just not as clever as the rest
      plus people think I'm a pest
       and I try not to make a mess
        it's just I wanted my name to be Jess
         I wish I could sink to the bottom of Loch Ness.

        I always order a takeaway
         I wish they could take me away
          Instead of playing pay day
           I wish I could shout May day

           My life is tangled in a web
            as I dangle
             why do I try?

Georgia Quinn (10)
Claremont Primary School

Monkey Business

M ysterious
O bstacle
N aughty monkey
K ind
E nchanting
Y ipee, monkey

B aldy belly
U nknown type
S illy nonsense
I rritating,
N othing
E lse, is like the
S ense a monkey has.
S illy monkey at Edinburgh Zoo.

Chloe McKenna (10)
Claremont Primary School

Football

F ootball is a great game.
O nly when it does not rain.
O f course there are goals.
T he celebrations are forward rolls.
B ecause it's 90 minutes.
A ll people want to win it.
L ittle people are very fast.
L ook at him going past.

Football's my favourite game.
Is it yours too?

Gary Martin (10)
Claremont Primary School

My Brother

My brother Matthew is pretty cool
He likes to jump in the swimming pool.

My brother Matthew is footie mad
But sometimes he gets very bad.

My brother Matthew is kind of goofy
He jumps about and makes his hair loopy.

My brother Matthew watches telly
And eats all the jelly.

My brother Matthew is soft and gentle
Sometimes he gets very mental.

My brother Matthew is a funky guy
Sometimes he dreams he can fly.

My brother Matthew got stuck up a tree
And he did a wee.

My brother Matthew is pretty cool
He likes to jump in the swimming pool.

Lauren McQueenie (10)
Claremont Primary School

Me, Myself And I

Me, myself and I are lazy,
Me, myself and I like pepperoni,
Me, myself and I like Daisy,
Me, myself and I are moany.

Me, myself and I are kind,
Me, myself and I are messy,
Me, myself and I are behind,
Me, myself and I are all dressy.

Emma Chalmers (10)
Claremont Primary School

My Crazy Dad

My dad is crazy,
He jumps about the room,
Upstairs, doon stairs,
And doon the toon,
He sounds pretty weird,
Like he's got glasses and a beard,
But actually he's quite nice,
Even though his breath stinks of rice.

I really do love him
And he loves me too,
But it's embarrassing when he hops about,
Like a kangaroo.

Emma McDowall (10)
Claremont Primary School

My Brother

My brother is one, he is dumb,
My brother is two, he smells like poo,
My brother is three, he looks like me,
My brother is four, he knocks on my door,
My brother is five, he likes to drive,
My brother is six, he hits my hips,
My brother is seven, he is at Heaven,
My brother is eight, he has no mates,
My brother is nine, he is mine,
My brother is ten, he can draw with a pen
     And that's my brother Jake.

Stephanie Forbes (10)
Claremont Primary School

My Family

My mum is thin
My dad is fat
I am slim
And so is my cat!

My fish is chubby
My parrot's a state
My dog is fluffy
My gran is great!

But most of all
Inside my house
I love this pet
It is my mouse.

I know it's weird
But that is that
I think I'll go
And pat my cat.

Vhari McClements (10)
Claremont Primary School

My Family

My family is supportive
They care for me a lot

My dad is funny, warm and cuddly
My mum is loving and caring
My brother is supportive, kind and fun.

We all say stupid things,
But my family make it better,
They all surprise me good and bad.

But there's one thing I know
My family are priceless,
Something I can't buy.

Sarah Dick (10)
Claremont Primary School

My Family

My family is so nice
For all my life.
And I will always love them.
My mum, dad and sister.
I love them more than anyone else.
Love is what you say to them.
You will always love your family.

Gavin Doig (10)
Claremont Primary School

Animals

Animals are cute
Animals are fun
But they can be dumb

Animals are cheerful
Animals are playful
And they can be fateful

Animals are good
Animals eat food
But they can be rude

Animals are great
Animals have fate
And they can be a mate

Animals are cool
Animals don't go to school
I like *animals!*

Shannon Cunningham (10)
Claremont Primary School

Best Friend

B y the way you're my best friend
E very day I play with you
S omeone tries to take you away
T ell someone, that's what I do

F riends are trustworthy
R ight away I knew
I like my best friend and she likes me too
E verybody knows exactly what we do
N obody falls out
D o you know we never do?

Kirsty Macaulay (10)
Claremont Primary School

Dirtbiking

Dirtbiking is fun,
You better not ride with a gun,
You better not break a leg,
Or you will be in a bed.
It is very dear,
So don't break your gears,
Or you will lose your ears.
Don't hit a stone,
Or you will break a bone.
Don't snap your handlebars
And don't crash into cars,
And don't eat lots of chocolate bars.
Or you will put on weight and go slow,
And you will not be able to go.

Craig Weir (10)
Claremont Primary School

My Maniac Mum

It's not the way she dances round and round,
It's not that her feet don't touch the ground,
It's not the way she says hello,
It's not the way she makes a bellow,
It's not the way she jumps up high,
It's not the way her head's in the sky.

It's definitely not the way she thinks,
It's definitely not the way she winks,
It's surely not the way she talks,
It's obviously not the way she walks,
I'm sure it's something in her belly,
Maybe it's the wobbly jelly?
Of course it's not, it's maybe me,
Or perhaps she's just a busy bee.

It's not the way she looks about,
It's not the way she catches trout,
It's not that she thinks the garage is a stable,
It's not the way she sets the table,
It's not the way her teeth chatter,
It's not the way she asks the matter.

It's not the way she's pretty cool,
It's not that she jumps in the swimming pool,
It's not that she can't climb a tree,
It's not that she doesn't look after me.

It is the fact that she's my mum,
It is the fact she likes to hum,
It is the fact she can't sing in tune,
It is the fact she was born in June.

Emma Johnstone (10)
Claremont Primary School

My Mum

My mum is kind,
My mum is pretty,
My mum is young,
My mum is caring,
I love my mum.

My mum is great,
You're my mum,
You're my mate.

My family loves her,
You should love her too,
My mum is the best person
In the whole world.

In my mind my mum is kind,
She is beautiful
And if you don't think so,
You're so blind!

The marriage of my mum and dad
Happened 14 years ago
Everyone went to the wedding.

Be nice to my mum
Everyone be nice
So if you don't like my mum
Tell me why?

She's simply the best!

Rebecca Wilson (10)
Claremont Primary School

Take A Nap

(Based on 'Cats Sleep Anywhere' by Eleanor Farjeou)

Cats sleep anywhere,
Any table, any chair,
Top of piano,
Window ledge,
In the middle,
Or the edge,
Try to fit in a cardboard box,
Or any lap will do.

Hannah O'Connor (10)
Claremont Primary School

Animals Endangered

A lways keep the animals alive because,
N othing is worse than killing an animal,
I n a bumblebee's hive,
M ajor incidents has the crocodile,
A nd he always swims in the River Nile,
L ies at the bottom like an old ship owner,
S pecial animals should be cared for,

E ndangered animals are mostly in the wild,
N ot like a rabbit that is mild,
D on't fling your rubbish down,
A nywhere at all,
N ot in the park, down town or in the mall,
G o to the forest and help all of the animals before,
E ndangered animals are dead,
R espect the animals instead of hurting them and,
E nd up as an expert,
D o a good job by picking up the litter.

All of the animals should be cared for.

Lyndsay Graham (10)
Claremont Primary School

Smoking's Bad For You

S moking is out of order
M aking life an awful lot harder
O pen arguing till life is gone
K illing you part by part
I n and out it goes
N ot a breath to take
G o on stop for goodness sake
S ome people say you may be right

B ut you know it is wrong
A wful changes to your life
D on't let them make you smoke

F orgot that you have a life
O r don't like the way you live
R egret it once you've done it

Y ou may be right, you may be wrong.
O pen your eyes and see
U ngrateful so you are.

Julie-Anne Mullady (10)
Claremont Primary School

My Big Sister

My big sister is a pest, she always looks her best,
Her music goes boom in her room,
My friends think she's nice, but she's made out of spice,
I like playing ball and she's a hundred feet tall,
She acts like the boss and I just get cross,
I'm bored and that's five goals she's scored,
My mum thinks she's good, but I know she's rude,

Now we're getting a row!

Amy Judge (10)
Claremont Primary School

Football

F ootball is my favourite sport
O h yes! What a goal!
O h another goal!
T ime for me to go play football with friends
B ombs away!
A way to the back of the net
L ovely goal
L eaping for joy!

Andrew Gibson (10)
Claremont Primary School

The Witch's Cat

Black, shiny, slick cat,
With a long, curly tail.
Claws like knives, eyes like the moon,
Creeping to catch his prey.
The best 'hisser' in town,
Gazing at the sky.

Andrew Forbes (8)
Cleish Primary School

The Witch's Cat

The black witch's cat,
Sneaking round the country in the dead of night.
Hypnotic eyes glowing like torches,
Razor-sharp claws to dig into victims.
Thin, black tail swishing in the night.
He sleeps soundly, with a gentle purr.

Ruaridh Stevenson (8)
Cleish Primary School

The View From My Window

The yellow corn sways gently in the breeze,
Pink rose, bay, willow and herbs surround the field,
Alongside the brownish dock
Which looks like it has been set on fire.

Over the river the golfers murmur,
Hoping to hole their shots in one.
Facing them the West Lomond Hill,
High and tall,
And nearby the slopes of the Bishop Hill.

Lewis Hunter (9)
Cleish Primary School

At The Funfair Ground

There I was at the funfair ground,
Bright flashing lights blasting like a concert,
The roller coaster swinging,
The bumper cars crashing,
The people screaming from the ghost train.

I heard the music jangling,
I saw the big dipper plunging down,
I smelt diesel fuel from the generator,
I tasted the popcorn,
I loved the fun of the fairground.

Stuart Hunter (11)
Cleish Primary School

At The Fair

The dodgems crashing and bashing,
The Ferris wheel spinning round in the sky,
The smell of hamburgers and onions drifting through the air.
People screaming and shouting with joy,
The generators humming along with the rides.
Happy and tired I go home to bed.

Adam Cunningham (9)
Cleish Primary School

A Trip To The Fair

I enter the bustling fair,
Ghastly smells from the powerful generators overwhelm me,
I am starting to feel hungry,
The odd whiff of freshly fried chips and onions meet my nostrils,
Hot dogs and hamburgers are being cooked on a barbecue,
Its smoke pollutes the air.
I start to munch on a toffee apple which I have won.

The fairground music is blaring in my ears,
Which ride should I go on first?
The big dipper or the swing boat?
My mouth becomes dry as I sit in one of the glittering waltzer cars.
I feel sick!

I start to climb up the stairs of the helter skelter,
Towering above the minute people,
I zoom down, down, down.
I walk towards the murky carriages of the ghost train.
My stomach churns,
I step off the ghost train and look at my watch.
It is time to go,
I feel happy and I have enjoyed today.
Do I have to go?
I love the fair!

Catriona Blair (10)
Cleish Primary School

Vandalism Is Bad

Unhappy Mum and Dad
Vandalism makes them mad!
It is a stupid thing to do
And it ruins the community too.

Ryan Petrie (8)
Crail Primary School

Community

C aring
O ld people
M arvellous
M agic
U nited
N eighbourly
 I nteresting
T idy
Y oung people.

Michelle Murray (8)
Crail Primary School

Litter

Litter is not nice.
It could make the town get mice.
Dropping litter is terrible.
It makes the place smell horrible.
Dropping litter is bad.
It could make people sad.
Litter is rubbish.
So are bones of fish.
Dropping litter ruins the environment.
We should tell the government.

Laura Wilson (8)
Crail Primary School

Sean's Community Poem

C rail
O rdinary
M agic
M agnificent
U nited
N ice
I nteresting
T idy
Y oung.

Sean Barnes (8)
Crail Primary School

Desert Mornings

As the day breaks
The sky turns bright.
The colour of the sky
Is like red roses and purple pansies.
The cacti silhouetted black
Stand like hairy hands
Coming out of the ground.

Rebecca Grieve (10)
Crail Primary School

The Community

C aring Crail
O ur community
M uffled
M erry
U nselfish
N eat
I mpressive
T actful
Y oung.

Blair Watson (8)
Crail Primary School

Desert Ocean

A waterless sea of barren waves,
Frozen as if time has stopped.
The humpbacked ships
Drowned by golden water
As it flew in a raging storm.
But now, deadly calm, the waves are still.
Those who sailed there lost,
Their choked corpses hidden,
All except one vine-entangled arm,
Raised above the bone dry waves,
Calling, crying, cautioning.

Alice Rhodes (10)
Crail Primary School

Desert Nights

D esert nights come and go,
E very night is lifeless.
S ome can't stand the heat;
E very day an animal dies.
R ound the desert,
T o try and find water.

N o one to be found,
I n the hot desert nights.
G o in peace and find
H appiness somewhere;
T o find happiness go anywhere,
S o find somewhere . . . but the desert.

Chloe Forsyth (10)
Crail Primary School

Desert

Day breaks
On a warm desert morning.
The sun rises on the horizon
And the sky turns pink, purple and yellow.
The cacti stand tall and still,
Black against the rising sun,
Like hands growing through the ground.

Bryony Harper (10)
Crail Primary School

The Desert

The dissimilar shades of orange sand
Cover the desert floor.
As a warm breeze drifts across the azure sky,
The sand dunes move
And make different shapes and sizes.
A brown snake with black and blood-red dashes
Moves sideways across the wasteland floor.

Katie Wilson (10)
Crail Primary School

The Desert

The desert sky is calm and colourful,
With its purples, yellows and even pinks.
And the desert skies have never seen rain.
But on the floor of the desert there is water,
But not much to be seen.

Nicole Petrie (10)
Crail Primary School

Desert Morning

As dawn breaks,
On a scorching summer morning,
With the prickly cacti getting warmer,
The sun rises on the horizon
With its citrus colours
Glowing over the still grass,
With not a breeze to be seen,
As the beautiful coloured snakes
Slither through the grass.

Kirsten McKay (10)
Crail Primary School

The Child

Some children are quite unique
But this child is very unique
He cries for food and water
He does not have shelter
He is the one that needs help the most.

Kelvin Budd (11)
Crail Primary School

Polar Winter

The polar winter has come.
The Arctic waters are cold,
And the frosty mountains are white,
Reflecting the sun's cool light.

On the cold, cold snow,
All alone, with no one beside him,
An upright polar bear sits,
Clasping in his powerful paw
A slimy fish, wriggling and raw.

Joanne Stockwell (10)
Crail Primary School

A Child

A child could be happy, fun and bright
A child could be stubborn and start a fight

A child could be poor and live on the street
A child could be wealthy and eat lots of meat

A child could be healthy, have fun and play
A child could be sick and ill all day

A child could be a twin and sound the same
A child could be an only and have some shame

There are different children all around.

Emily Paterson (11)
Crail Primary School

The Child On The Street

See the child lying on the street
With only a thin blanket and some ragged clothes.
Some cheap food and half a bottle of water
Some money lying in front of him but not a lot
Still it is enough to buy some food and drink
To keep him alive.

James Stewart (11)
Crail Primary School

Community

C rail is clean
R eally good
A caring community
I t is fantastic
L ovely place to live.

Lucy Chalmers (8)
Crail Primary School

Community

C aring Crail is beautiful.
O ur community is helpful.
M aths is what we do at school.
M useum tells us about old Crail.
U nited people are in our town.
N eighbourly people get along.
 I nteresting Crail is nice to live in.
T asty crabs and lobsters down at the harbour.
Y oung children like me are funny and playful.

Claire Thomson (8)
Crail Primary School

How An Aspiring Teenager Reacts

An aspiring teenager reacts in a strop
When her sister makes an ornament drop.
An aspiring teenager reacts in a roar
When her brother makes her perfume pour.
An aspiring teenager reacts in a blow
When her mum says, 'No! You can't go.'
An aspiring teenager reacts in a rage
When her dad says, 'You can't drink, you're under age!'
An aspiring teenager reacts like a bomb
When her best friend goes out with Tom.
An aspiring teenager is me!

Katie Clayton (11)
Crail Primary School

Night And Day

In the day the trains roar
People come more and more
The cold seats are always full
And someone's left a ball of wool.

In the night there is no light
But just an eerie sound
It was the howling of a dog
And that's just what I found.

In the day the trains are full
I took my dog she gave me a pull
Suddenly I was on a train
The train stopped at the plane.

Night has come
I'm very cold
The planes look very dark
And old.

Then something comes up behind
But I think it's just my mind
Then I realise it's a plane
I jump on board as it started to rain.

I thought as my home
Came into sight
Maybe I won't
Go out at night!

Fiona Cuthill (10)
Creich Primary School

The Modern Turtle

Two hundred turtles sleeping on the sand,
Oompah! Oompah! went the brass band.
What's the brass band about? I hear you all say.
The modern turtle wanted to be different, not the same,
All he ever wanted was to have some fame.
He had a wave come over him, the brain kind not the sea,
He wanted to be coloured but dad would not agree.
Being a teenager turtle you know what I mean,
He explained to his dad the importance of being seen.
With Daddy now won over, he told him his idea,
The very same day, some paints were washed up from Ikea!
The pair of them brushed and glossed all through the night,
Two hundred turtles were soon to see a most amazing fight.
Gold, silver, indigo, blue more than I can tell,
Colours never seen before were covering his shell.
A party had to be arranged on the golden sand,
Oompah! Oompah! went the brass band.

Hayley Rees (11)
Creich Primary School

In The Dungeons

In the dungeons are
Lots of ghosts ooo ooo oooing!
Skeletons rattling!
A monster in chains, roaring!
A witch cackling!
Trolls stamping!
Goblins laughing!
Devils blowing fire
And mice chewing!
Rats scratching
And thunder crashing!
Wolves howling
And dragons blowing fire!
Dinosaurs growling
And bats fluttering!
The quietest thing was
The spiders creep, creep, creeping!

Mhairi Roberts (8) & Hannah Fricke (7)
Creich Primary School

Haunted House

In the cellar is . . .
a decaying hangman's noose
a horde of hungry rats
a pile of flesh covered bones
a bag of old rusty knives
and the only sound that could be heard
was the squeaking rats.

In the attic is . . .
an old rusty bike with no wheels
a lot of scuttling spiders
a dusty pile of boxes
a dusty old globe spinning
and the only sound is the globe spinning.

In the dining room is . . .
an old oak table
with eight chairs creaking in the wind
a skeleton sat at the head of the table
but his head was on the floor
and the only sound was bones
creaking in the wind.

James Barker (11)
Creich Primary School

The Worm

The worm
slithers
underground
and
pops its
slimy head
up with two
gleaming
eyes
it leaves
its slimy
track on the
grass
as it finds
its
way
home.

Craig Roberts (11)
Creich Primary School

In The Factory

In the factory it roars,
The monster machine
Crunches its victims flat.

I bravely went into its darkness,
It roared louder than ever before,
I screamed in terror.

I ran out of its darkness,
It grabbed me and pulled me
Into its lair.

Euan Stewart (11)
Dunbog Primary School

The Chimney

'Sweep that chimney now boy'
Anxiously I climbed to the roof
I saw the long, dark, gloomy tunnel ahead of me
The emptiness roared, I climbed inside.

The murky depths were dark, as dark could be
I sneezed, I wheezed
Things fell
I slipped; I jarred my legs into the wall.

The pepper fell into my mouth
It tasted like rotting flea powder
A roar of the dragon
Flare of flames fried my feet.

I scrambled up that horrid tunnel
Air fizzed through my hair
My feet were fried like toast.

Donald Stewart (11)
Dunbog Primary School

Down The Mine

Down the mine we go,
Satan's children slaving away at the stone of grief.
Digging at sorrow, which brings sadness to many
And good to none.
The little spirits gnawing at the rock
Never to see the light of day again,
Hell has come,
Satan is here,
There is no escape from the blood stricken terror!

Christian Smith (10)
Dunbog Primary School

Down In The Dark

Down in the dark screaming mines,
Hell has arrived and never will leave,
Down in the dark evil mines,
The darkness wrapped around them.

Down in the dark harsh mines,
Injury and death is popular,
Down in the dark dirty mines,
Satan is down there.

Down in the dark treacherous mines,
Everyone hates it,
Down in the dark gloomy mines,
The horrible disliked place.

Down in the dark screaming mines,
Down in the dark screaming mines,
Down in the dark, dark hell.

Robert Struthers (10)
Dunbog Primary School

The Mine

Down in the deep, dark, black, smelly mine,
Where no one dares to go,
There is a path that some people call the path of death,
Few people walk through the path of death and return.
The children pray for freedom,
Sleep and to see their family and their friends
One more time before they die.

Chloe Gordon (7)
Dunbog Primary School

To The Beginning Of Hell

I went to the beginning of Hell
To the only place I didn't want to be,
And the only place I'm going.
The darkness took me
Into the Devil's chamber,
I stepped into darkness,
The maggoty wood above me roared,
The mist came and I couldn't breathe,
The darkness took me,
The darkness took me,
The darkness took me forever.

Ben Kerridge (11)
Dunbog Primary School

My Favourite Senses

My favourite sound is . . .
Birds chirping in the trees.
My friends talking the playground.

My favourite feeling is . . .
Cool water trickling on my hand.
My furry cats.

My favourite sight is . . .
A nice picture in my book.
Sun sparkling on the sea.

My favourite taste is . . .
A big cheeseburger
And sizzling bacon.

My favourite smell is . . .
Hot chocolate with marshmallows.
Ice cream - cold and sweet.

Sean Sirur (7)
Dysart Primary School

My Favourite Senses

My favourite sounds . . .
Crashing of thunder,
Humming of the birds.

My favourite feelings . . .
Hot quilt on a cold day,
Tickly feelings when a spider
Runs up my hand.

My favourite sights . . .
The late sunset,
The high view from a cliff.

My favourite smells . . .
A hot cup of tea,
A hot chilli.

My favourite tastes . . .
Sticky toffee,
Sweet strawberries.

Gary Paterson (7)
Dysart Primary School

My Favourite Senses

My favourite sounds are . . .
The banging of books as they slam.
The splash of light water.

My favourite feelings are . . .
Big crunchy doughnuts in my hands.
Cold, wet water spilling all over me.

My favourite sights are . . .
Fat greasy hamburgers.
Small brown Yorkie bars.

My favourite smells are . . .
Hot tasty shortbread cakes in the oven.
Hot crispy pancakes baking.

Brian Smith (7)
Dysart Primary School

My Favourite Senses

My favourite sound is . . .
foxes howling
and Lego smashing.

My favourite feeling is . . .
a nice cup of tea
and nice cat fur.

My favourite sight is . . .
the sea sparkling
and nice sun in the sky.

My favourite tastes are . . .
nice toffee apples
and candyfloss.

My favourite smell is . . .
a spicy Chinese
and air fresheners.

Rory Smith (7)
Dysart Primary School

House Dreams

The Gamecube reminds me of entertainment.
The cat can hear me speak in cat language.
The window dislikes birds pooping on it
And the house dreams that it stays up forever.

The fridge is worried if it gets too full of food.
My bedroom loves me and my family.
My parents' bedroom loves my mum's clothes
And the house dreams it was a nightclub.

Aarron Balfour (11)
Dysart Primary School

My Mum

Mum is a Sagittarius,
She was born in December,
She tells us to tidy our room
But we don't remember.

When I give her a cuddle,
She feels like a koala bear,
She always smells nice
Around her soft hair.

Ross Leslie (10)
Dysart Primary School

The Wind

When the wind is howling between the buildings
It is a wolf desperately searching for its lost cubs.
When the wind is whispering through the trees
It is a snake silently creeping to its den.
When the wind is making a cold draught in the house
It is a lion angrily roaring at its prey.
When the wind is flickering flames in a fire
It is a honeybee guarding its beehive.
When the wind is blowing umbrellas inside out
It is an elephant unsteadily falling to the ground.
When the wind is carrying a dandelion seed along
It is a bird gently flapping its wings to get to its cosy nest.
When the wind is breaking branches off a tree
It is a rhino loudly sneezing.

Christina Sinclair (10)
Dysart Primary School

Valentine's Day

Valentine's Day
All about love
Special birds for the day
Called doves.

You think Valentine's Day is mush
But maybe, just maybe you have a crush
You smile at him with big googly eyes
He smiles at you and you're surprised

He comes up to you to give you a kiss
Your day is so full, full of bliss
So now you know, please won't you say
That you love every bit of Valentine's Day.

Valentine's Day
All about love
Special birds for the day
Called doves.

Natalie Galloway (11)
Dysart Primary School

Anteater

Anteater, anteater,
Can't eat plants.
Anteater, anteater,
Can eat ants!

Anteater, anteater,
Stick out your tongue.
Anteater, anteater,
Look what has clung!

Anteater, anteater,
Under your snout.
The ants go in
But don't come out!

Gaby Leslie (8)
Dysart Primary School

Bad Memories

When newly born he slept a lot.
He cried often at night like most babies do.
Was sick on me
And dribbled on my chin.
Got lots of presents while I got none.

Now he fights with Mitchell-Jay
And eats my food.
Plays the PlayStation
Untidies my room.
He broke my bird's perch and laughed and ran away.
Jumps on the couch he gets a row from Mum.

But - he is my wee brother and I love him.

Toni Walton (11)
Dysart Primary School

Chocolate

Chocolate is good
Chocolate is yummy.
Chocolate is tasty
For my tummy.

Chocolate is long
Chocolate is square
If it melts
It goes everywhere.

It comes in eggs
It comes in bars
And also comes
In sweetie jars.

Mmmm . . . chocolate!

Emma Wilson (10)
Dysart Primary School

The Amazing Colours Of Blue

The blazing blue sky just sitting with not a care in the world
with seagulls fighting over chips.
The hot sun setting on the clear sea,
the mountain as big as the clouds and for all to see,
soft blue silk that is very long, that is blue.

Joshua Wilkinson (10)
Dysart Primary School

Ma Maw

My maw is awfully crabby
She never shuts her mooth
If she shouts at me again
I'll knock her through the roof.

But I've got to admit
She's got a lovely cheesy grin
And I just love her two fat chins!

Ma maw's rather fat
She looks like a plum
The chair's two wee
It doesn'ae fit her bum.

But . . .
Ma maw does a' ma washing
Does ma ironing too.
She's no a bad cook
I just love her stew

Ma maw is always happy
I love her cheery smile
And when I fall and hurt ma knee
For her cuddles I'd run a mile!

Kerry Lister (11)
Dysart Primary School

Animals

When the wind is howling between the buildings
it is a wolf desperately searching for its lost cubs.
When the wind is whispering
it's a snake looking for its food.
When the wind is making a cold draught in the house
it is a lion sneaking up behind you
giving you the cold shivers.
When the wind is flickering flames in a fire
it's a phoenix flying high.
When the wind is blowing umbrellas inside out
it's a tiger roaring loud.

Keighley Paterson (10)
Dysart Primary School

The World Around Us

When the wind is howling between the buildings
It is a wolf, desperately searching for its lost cubs.

When the wind is whispering in the trees
I see a snake sneaking up on its prey.

When the wind is cold and slimy
I think of a jelly eel desperately trying to crawl back to the sea.

When the wind is growling and roaring,
It is a wolf cub raging playfully.

When the wind is gently blowing,
It is a mother bear silently rocking her cubs to sleep.

When the wind is blowing at the fire,
It is a phoenix burning to make new life.

When the wind is breaking branches off a tree,
It is a woodpecker pecking at the tree.

Danielle Cunningham (10)
Dysart Primary School

Simile Poem

How to make a dessert you need . . .

A bowl like a banana.
A strawberry as red as a fire alarm.
An orange like a fire.
A flake like a tree trunk.
Ice cream like a big snowball.
Grapes like my green jotter.
Swiss roll like a round rubber.

Gemma Morrison (10)
Dysart Primary School

The Animal Poem

When the wind is howling between the buildings
it is a wolf, desperately searching for its lost cubs.
When the wind is gently whispering through the trees
it is a lizard, looking for food.
When the wind is making a cold draught in the house
it is a polar bear, it is sliding down the ice down into the water.
When the wind is flickering flames in a fire it is a bird,
flapping its beautiful, lovely blue wings.
When the wind is blowing umbrellas inside out
it is a hippo blowing very hard.
When the wind is carrying a dandelion seed along
it is a wasp stinging people.
When the wind is breaking branches off a tree
it is a monkey eating delicious appetising yellow bananas.

Darrel Johnston (10)
Dysart Primary School

The Strong Wind

When the wind is howling between the buildings
it is a wolf, desperately searching for its lost cubs.
When the wind is whispering through the trees
it is a snake, slithering around, looking for its prey.
When the wind is making a cold draught in the house
it is an elephant, blowing cold air from its long trunk.
When the wind is flickering flames in a fire
it is a bee, pausing in the air looking for flowers,
to collect nectar to make tasty honey.
When the wind is blowing umbrellas inside out
it is a lion, roaring at the other big lion.
When the wind is carrying a dandelion seed along
it is a gorilla, panting because he has been running that fast.
When the wind is breaking branches off a tree
it is a reindeer, that heavy it breaks the thin branches.

Kayleigh Bannerman (10)
Dysart Primary School

My Favourite Senses

My favourite sound is the engine of a stock car.
My favourite smell is air fresheners.
My favourite feeling is my smooth cheek.
My favourite sight is a tricycle.
My favourite sight is my mum's home-made soup.

Alex Mill (7)
Dysart Primary School

My Favourite Senses

My favourite sounds are . . .
Thunder and lightning crashing
And bacon sizzling.

My favourite to touch is . . .
The feeling of fluffy cushions
Soft and smooth.

My favourite sights are . . .
The sight of the river bank
When I look out my window I see the sun rise.

My favourite tastes . . .
I like the taste of dipping my Twix in a cup of tea,
The taste of macaroni.

My favourite smells . . .
I like the smell of my tea when it is ready,
I like the smell of apple crumble.

Dylan Anderson (7)
Dysart Primary School

It Was So Quiet That . . .

It was so quiet that . . .
I heard another galaxy rumbling
away in the distance.
I heard the man in the moon
sing in the shower.
I heard the dark night
rush through the house.

Lucy Nash (9)
Greyfriars RC Primary School

It Was So Quiet That . . .

It was so quiet that . . .
I heard Tutankhamen snoring in his sarcophagus
I heard a grey mouse eating his orange cheese
I heard the moon talking to the twinkling stars
I heard the penguins having a chat at the South Pole
I heard ants marching into battle in the distance
I heard a rocket up in space
I heard a spider spinning its web
I heard workers building pyramids in Egypt
I heard people having a dinner party in New Zealand
I heard the planets spinning in space.

Oliver Grieve (8)
Greyfriars RC Primary School

It Was So Quiet That . . .

It was so quiet that . . .
I heard the flowers singing in the noisy garden.
I heard the moon chatting to the gossiping stars.
I heard the houses groaning with tiredness.
I heard the snow fluttering down.
I heard the dolphins shimmering under the sea.
I heard Santa opening presents at Christmas.

Courtney Thom (8)
Greyfriars RC Primary School

It Was So Quiet That . . .

It was so quiet that . . .
I heard a centipede stomping across the wooden floor.
I heard a wall sobbing at an evil nail.
I heard the leaves falling from the sad tree.
I heard Re snoring when he was sleeping in the sun.
I heard a buzzy bee buzzing.
I heard the sun burning the grass.
I heard a butterfly fluttering.
I heard Pluto moving around the sun.

Dily Mordi (8)
Greyfriars RC Primary School

You

You!
Your mouth is like a squirming, wriggling worm.
You!
Your toes are like pink, glowing glow-worms.
You!
Your face is like a round, chubby coconut.
You!
Your armpits smell like odorous sewer rats.
You!
Your skin is green, spotted like an island in the sea.

Jonathan Watson (8)
Greyfriars RC Primary School

Things Found In Smeagol's Pockets

The one ring to rule them all.
Fish bones.
Finger of Frodo.
False teeth.
ID to get into Mordor.
Picture of the fat one and darts.
Fishing rod.
Piece of paper saying the fat one's stupid.
Fish.
Hair extenders.
Breath freshener.
Cough sweets.

Harvey Leicester (8)
Greyfriars RC Primary School

Things You Would Find In Pippin's Pocket

A packet of mints.
A small sword.
A map of Hobbiton.
An A-Z book of elvish.
A bag of rocks for weapons.
Some spare shoes.
A bottle of water.
Some elvish bread with butter.
A small teddy bear
And a fluffy hat.

Andro Mathewson (8)
Greyfriars RC Primary School

It Was So Quiet That . . .

It was so quiet that . . .
I heard the leaves falling from the sad tree.
I heard the rats whispering in dark, deep places.
I heard the eagle swooping up and down in the sky.
I heard the butterfly's wings fluttering.
I heard the angel praying in Heaven.
I heard the fish in the blue sea shimmering up and down.
I heard the red volcano rumbling in the dark night.
I heard the sunlight's sparkle on the sea.

Francesca Baldacchino (9)
Greyfriars RC Primary School

It Was So Quiet That . . .

It was so quiet that . . .
I heard the moon go around the Earth
I heard the sand wave millions of miles away
I heard the monkey climbing a tree.
I heard the water in a calm river.
I heard the tree bleeding down its spine.
I heard all the planets swirling around the sun.
I heard the fish swimming alone in the water.
I heard the rumble from the core of the Earth.
I heard the rugby World Cup.
I heard the war in Iraq.

Lewis Rae (9)
Greyfriars RC Primary School

It Was So Quiet That . . .

It was so quiet that . . .
I heard the planets zoom round the sun.
I heard the dead people whoosh up to Heaven.
I heard crinkled leaves crashing to the dry ground.
I heard the dust fly across the dry ground.
I heard the squeak of a mouse in the next-door house.
I heard the cry of Indians charging through the forest.
I heard angry ants running to the cave.
I heard the pyramids crumbling in Egypt.
I heard snakes slither silently across shrivelled grass.
I heard shells smash at the deepest and darkest part of the sea.
I heard Philip Think talking to Baby B.
I heard an avalanche smashing houses down in Australia.
I heard the cry of drowning sailors.

Dougal MacEwan (8)
Greyfriars RC Primary School

It Was So Quiet That . . .

It was so quiet that . . .
I heard a piece of black bark falling from the tree.
I heard the snow blasting from the sky.
I heard a piece of lead melting on the sunbeams.
I heard leaves falling from the bare tree.
I heard people making papyrus.
I heard water whooshing through the pipes.
I heard the lead screech on a piece of paper.

Connor Morrison
Greyfriars RC Primary School

It Was So Quiet That . . .

It was so quiet that . . .
I heard the Egyptian gods playing board games.
I heard the torrential storms on Jupiter.
I heard the navy shooting missiles out to sea.
I heard the pharaoh whispering to his mummified cat.
I heard my own blood going round my body.
I heard the Vikings charging into battle.
I heard the sound of rushing water in Africa.
I heard the aliens laughing on Mars.
I heard a shark sensing human flesh.
I heard Gollum thinking about his precious ring
In the rocky wasteland.

Oliver Cocris (8)
Greyfriars RC Primary School

You!

You!
Your hair is like a tangled, stinky rat's nest.
You!
Your teeth are like smashed, huge rocks.
You!
Your mouth is like a black, dark bear's cave.
You!
Your eyes are like balls of green sewer water.
You!
Your skin is like rotten green scales.

Michal Martin (9)
Greyfriars RC Primary School

It Was So Quiet That . . .

It was so quiet that . . .
I heard the bark falling off the weeping tree.
I heard the stars shoot through the dark night.
I heard the blossom sprout from their tiny buds.
I heard the rubber dust crash to the wooden floor.
I heard the beams of the sun shimmer on the softly cut grass.
I heard the water trickle in a small pond.

Sadie Irving (8)
Greyfriars RC Primary School

You!

You!
Your eyes are like large round pigeon holes.
You!
Your teeth are like white, bumpy, wrapped up mummies.
You!
Your beard is like a grey dusty fireplace.
You!
Your ears are like a waxy yellow bog.
You!
Your neck is like skinny thin lamp posts.
You!
Your skin is like a flaky beach ball.

Bridie Lamb (8)
Greyfriars RC Primary School

You!

You!
Your hair is like knotted rats' tails.
You!
Your eyes are like 2 pencil pots.
You!
Your hands are like 2 crusted pies.
You!
Your nose is like a tall jaggy mountain.
You!
Your bum is like 2 red apples.
You!
Your eyes are like boiling hot suns.

Jasmine King (8)
Greyfriars RC Primary School

You!

You!
Your hair is like an old bird's nest.
You!
Your eyes are like green fireballs.
You!
Your hands are like an old dusty book.
You!
Your fingers are like green little twigs.
You!
Your nails are like a yellow mouldy fish.

Emily Christianson (8)
Greyfriars RC Primary School

It Was So Quiet That . . .

It was so quiet that . . .
I heard my hair growing
I heard it snowing
I heard the moon singing
I heard the sun flinging its warmth upon the earth
I heard far away a mother giving birth
I heard myself blink
I heard my friend wink at me
I heard the fishes swimming at the bottom of the sea
I heard the leaves on the trees
I heard the birds fly in the blue sky
I heard the stars twinkling in the sky.

Natalie Northridge (8)
Greyfriars RC Primary School

It Was So Quiet That . . .

It was so quiet that . . .
I heard the leaves falling off the sad naked tree.
I heard my blood running through my body.
I heard my eardrum drumming in my ear.
I heard the rubber rubbering out.
I heard the snow falling down from the windy sky.
I heard the bees buzzing through the sky.

Courtney Gatherum (8)
Greyfriars RC Primary School

Autumn

Autumn
finally I
see leaves falling off trees
in the misty
mornings.

Kirsten McBride
Inverkeithing Primary School

Autumn

Autumn
golden leaves and
yellow too. Mornings are
chilly, misty
as well.

Simon Thomas (10)
Inverkeithing Primary School

Autumn

Autumn
is finally
here. Bare trees, crunchy leaves
very, very
chilly.

Chanise Harvey (10)
Inverkeithing Primary School

Autumn

Autumn
golden leaves fall
floating down to the ground
the leaves are gone
bare trees.

Aileen Simpson (10)
Inverkeithing Primary School

Autumn

Autumn
coming once a
year swirling burling leaves
crunching leaves all
the time.

Jessica Barrie (10)
Inverkeithing Primary School

Industrial Landscape

The
grubby
factories
puffing out smoke
into the dismal
grey sky with tall
black chimneys,
giants
all.

Ryan Williams (9)
Inverkeithing Primary School

Industrial Landscape

In
The black
Dull sky there
Is horrible
Smoke belching out of
Tall chimneys and
Polluting
The clear
Skies.

Greg Milne (10)
Inverkeithing Primary School

Autumn

Autumn
Finally I
See leaves falling again
From trees. I love
Autumn.

Emma Black (10)
Inverkeithing Primary School

Industrial Landscape

Skies
Are grey
Dark as coal
Tall chimneys stand
Puffing out dark smoke
Polluting towns
Causing dust
In the
Air.

Craig Melvin (10)
Inverkeithing Primary School

Industrial Landscape

Far
From here
Children and
Adults suffer
From the polluted skies.
The buildings dull
And the sky
Grey with
Smoke.

Carmel Wilkinson-Ayre (10)
Inverkeithing Primary School

Autumn's Death

Autumn,
It's the season of death.
Flowers wither, leaves die,
As I watch, I cry.

I clutch on to the trees,
Shaking.
As I watch the colours,
Fading.

You may think,
Why make such a fuss?
It's just autumn.
But I am Mother Nature,
And I know what is to come.

I listen to the leaves crunching,
Underneath your feet.
I think it is torture,
But you think it's a treat!

I must admit though,
I love the leaves so brown.
And the oranges and yellows,
Make no reason to frown.

Laura Watts (11)
Inverkeithing Primary School

Mother Nature

The crispy cold mornings have come knocking.

The lush green leaves are changing into burning reds and yellows
                                        and rusty dark browns.
They fall and then twist and turn like individual ballerinas in a show.
The time has come and the secrets of autumn are open.

From summer dresses and shorts, we change into long thick trousers.
Hats and scarves are coming into fashion.
So I guess autumn's here, loud and clear.

Autumn's here!

Rachael Barrie (11)
Inverkeithing Primary School

Now She's Gone

I see her in my shadow,
In my sleep too,
I always think of her,
Because I'm always blue,
And now she's gone.

Now she's gone, I'm all alone,
Nobody to talk to now,
She made me happy all the time,
And now she's gone.

I'm so lonely now she's gone,
As she was always laughing,
Always happy, her smiling, cheerful face,
But now she's gone.

Her hair was so soft,
It could have been used for a teddy bear,
Her perfume smelt of lavender and roses,
It reminded me of a meadow.

Aimee Minty (11)
Inverkeithing Primary School

Industrial Landscape

Sky
Grey, dull
Cloudy, dark
Black and dismal
Heaven white with smoke
Twirling, swirling
In the air
Death.

Jordan Sadler (10)
Inverkeithing Primary School

Autumn

The wind so cold and fresh,
The sky so light and dark,
The wall so hot or cold,
The clouds floating in the sky,
Towns so dark,
Gulls trying to get home,
Pipes so cold,
Shadows so dark,
The trees blowing in beat with the wind,
You can see houses from everywhere,
Pigeons so cold,
The leaves are cold and crunch when you touch them,
I can hear trains passing by,
The ground so cold,
Trees and crops trying to grow,
The smell, so sweet, of berries,
The fields dark and cold,
Metal so cold.

Catherine Ostrom (9)
Inverkeithing Primary School

Autumn

The wind is cold and strong like a block of ice,
The wind blows on your face,
The wind tastes like fresh air,
All the clouds are fluffy like bunnies' tails,
The air sounds like it is crying,
Half the sky is cloudy, half the sky is blue,
The walls feel like ice,
An aeroplane is flying to another place,
The river looks misty and cold,
All the trees blow as the wind goes by,
The light fills everything like sunrise,
The ground is freezing cold,
All the fields are harvested and ready for winter,
All the plants are dying,
It feels like winter already.

Holly Paterson (9)
Inverkeithing Primary School

Sound Poem

I heard popcorn pop,
My guinea pig squeaked,
Fireworks banged,
Cats miaowed,
Dogs woofed,
Coke fizzed,
I smashed a pot,
I gulped my tea down,
I crashed my bike into a car,
I pulled my zip down.

Natasha Briggs (9)
Inverkeithing Primary School

Sound Poem

You can hear a sound of a telephone ringing,
A clock ticking, and mooing in the background,
A buzzing noise from a bee,
Popcorn popping in the microwave,
You can hear cracking upstairs,
Fizzing juice when you open it,
Woofing in the backyard,
Splashing in the pool and sizzling bacon in the oven.

Fiona Hunter (9)
Inverkeithing Primary School

Guy Fawkes

Bangers explode like tanks in World War II,
Rockets bang in the air,
The colour sprays from Catherine wheels,
The children wave sparklers,
Pyramids spray out like fountains all over the grass,
People eat hot dogs while watching the parade.

Daniel Horn & Aidan Smith (9)
Inverkeithing Primary School

Fireworks

Loud banging in the sky
Screeching and whistling.
Rockets shoot into colours
Sparkling and glowing.
They burst into
Red, green and blue.

Hannah Masterton (7)
Inverkeithing Primary School

Fireworks

Loud banging filling the sky.
Whining in the air.
Exploding into colours.
Falling like rain.
Then it starts again.

Adam Parsley (7)
Inverkeithing Primary School

Fireworks

Screeching like an eagle.
Banging when it hits the sky.
They shoot up into the air.
Then they explode into lovely colours.
Star shapes and circles.
Sparkling and spinning.

Gavin Simpson (7)
Inverkeithing Primary School

Fireworks

Colours fall down like rain.
Glowing green and sparkling purple,
Showering down.
Dazzling red and orange stars,
Flying into the sky and exploding.
It bangs, and smoke comes down,
Filling the air with light.
Screeching like seagulls.

Taylor Galloway (7)
Inverkeithing Primary School

Fireworks

Fireworks explode into colours.
They crackle like gold,
And fall like rain,
Gold on the ground.
Another firework explodes into green,
Banging and screeching,
It fires into the air.

Christopher Ostrom (7)
Inverkeithing Primary School

Industrial Landscape

By
Dirty
Factories
Smoke is swirling
High above the trees.
Coughing, choking
Sometimes I
Cannot
Breathe.

Lesley Anne Reid (10)
Inverkeithing Primary School

Industrial Landscape

The
Smelly
Factories
Gruesome buildings
Smokey chimneys
Darkening
Clouds of
Grey.

Mark Cannon (10)
Inverkeithing Primary School

Industrial Landscape

The
Busy
Grey buildings
Black factories
Twisting smoke, climbing
Up to the sky
Pollution
Choking
Death.

Daniel Cameron (10)
Inverkeithing Primary School

Industrial Landscape

The
Dirty
Factories
Stand tall and grey.
From the huge chimneys
Puffing, twirling
Ghostly smoke
Drifting
Up.

Kyle Wright (10)
Inverkeithing Primary School

Velociraptor

Near a cave in a desert
Yellow eyes and deadly claws
Little dinosaurs escaping quickly
Chomp, chomp
Velociraptor.

David Wellsted (8)
Kennoway Primary & Community School

Autumn

Autumn changes all the time, leaves tumble down, weather
becomes bleak,
As combine harvesters cut and chomp the wheat.
Underneath the river lies the spectacular coloured trout,
Gouging holes for their young, tiny as an eye pupil.
Tremendous winds whirl everywhere, chilly climates,
Gloomy, thick fog follows, making everybody miserable.
Unstoppable fiery rockets, whizzing up into the murky night sky,
Crazy Catherine wheels gyrate like a car tyre going 1,000,000 miles
per hour.
Migrating birds soar smoothly across the gorgeous light blue sky,
Geese deafening us with musical wild cries, in orderly V-shaped
columns.
Natural colours of leaves, chocolate brown, lemon yellow, carrot
orange,
All blend together on the tips of the branches, looking like a bag
of sweets.

Jennifer Rankin (10)
Kennoway Primary & Community School

Winter

Winter is white trees full of snow
Winter is a grey sky with no sun
Winter is feeling shivery but happy
Winter is ice cracking
I like winter.

Dominic Curran (7)
Kennoway Primary & Community School

Winter

Winter is sparkly frost on the bare trees.
Winter is black ice in the playgrounds.
Winter is feeling cold and miserable.
Winter is wooshing sledges.
I don't like winter.

Abbie Staig (7)
Kennoway Primary & Community School

Autumn

Autumn weather, stormy gusts, gales, icy breezes
raindrops falling off roofs, getting less summer sunshine
cloudy days, thundering dark nights and windy mornings.
Umbrella, sloppy with rain pelting down on you
gigantic, deep, splashy puddles, getting drenched from
your head to your toes
dull, grey, cloudy skies.
Terrifying nightmares, creepy and weird, witches dancing
around cauldrons, ghosts alarming folk, spooky vampires,
killing, then sucking blood.
Under the dark sky, flashy, luminous fireworks, blazing
bonfires, sparkly, twinkling,
sparks flying,
colourful, crackly sparkles, booming rockets explode.
Moving, rustly, crispy, flaky fronds, topple
slowly, gently to the earth, colourful leaves
decorating the forest floor.
Neglected, elderly, aged tree, enormous, mouldy roots,
plump lofty trunks, twigs and stems covered with
sparkling white frost.

Hollie Ford (10)
Kennoway Primary & Community School

Autumn

Autumn, leaves falling, flutter like a suffering butterfly
Orange as the sparkling sun, red like roses.

Unhappy weather, rain like standing in a freezing blanket of water
Windy, a strong hairdryer blowing in your face.

The wonderful colours of the flaming bonfires spark all around
The fire crackling like sizzling bacon, snaps like crackers popping.

Unlike robins or sparrows, swallows fly to warm Africa
Geese arrive with musical honks, they like freezing weather.

Mini-beasts, bees and wasps will weaken and die,
No nectar left on flowers of plants.

Near Hallowe'en, witches, goblins, ghosts, devils,
Free to infest the dark, creep quietly around like working ants.

Megan Pullar (10)
Kennoway Primary & Community School

Winter

Winter is squelchy slush on the roads.
Winter is twinkling lights in houses.
Winter is feeling very cold and wet.
Winter is ice skates zinging.
    I love winter.

Tanya Charles (7)
Kennoway Primary & Community School

Autumn

Autumn,
empty fields like the desert,
tasty, luscious, delicious food lines the supermarket,
enjoyable, dainty, pleasing.
Undergrowth,
ruby-red leaves blazing like an inferno,
glistening gold, like a shimmering sun,
crisp, dry, colourful and brittle.
Tonight, fireworks fill the air with colour,
explosions, crackling sparklers, enjoyment, happiness,
excitement, monstrous bonfires burn splendidly.
Underneath swaying branches, agile squirrels frolic,
glossy berries, wonderful, amazing and beautiful,
a colourful world on the forest floor.
Many people become ill, doctors busy, chemists out of stock,
furry hats, gloves, blazing fires,
warm clothing, slippery icy frost.
Nights dark, damp, as black as winter,
dismal and opaque, scary shapes all around,
scared out of your wits.

Craig Docherty (10)
Kennoway Primary & Community School

Winter

Winter is silver ice on the rivers
Winter is glittery frost on black roads
Winter is pure white snow falling softly
Winter is feeling shivery and happy
Winter is owls hooting in dark nights
I like winter.

Sam Docherty (7)
Kennoway Primary & Community School

Stegosaurus

Near a swamp in a jungle
Plated back and tiny eyes
Ferns and long grass all around
Chomp, chomp
Stegosaurus.

Callum Hynd (7)
Kennoway Primary & Community School

Remembrance

R ed is the colour of the poppy's petals to symbolise the blood of
  the wounded soldiers.
E nemy tanks have death written all over them; emerge from a mist
  of chemical gases.
M isery showers all of those who never went to war, praying that their
  brothers, dads and friends will all come back.
E nemies charging like a stampede of antelope.
M assacred bodies lying all over the battlefield, while other soldiers
  flee.
B rave soldiers fight for their country, dying and killing. It's all
  slaughter.
R emember those who thought of their country before themselves.
A ngry, bitter men hobbled home.
N azis and Hitler are never forgiven.
C hildren screaming while bullets fly and people die.
E very year we remember those who died in the war.

Ian Fraser (11)
Kennoway Primary & Community School

Autumn

Autumn weather, foggy roads, blowing leaves,
icy winds like frozen ponds,
black clouds, frosty mornings,
crackling lightning.
Umbrellas, pounding rain, flooded as a lake,
trickling rain, soaking wet, sodden trousers,
damp skin, thundering clouds, terrifying gusts.
Travelling over land, journey north, noisy as a baby
crying,
geese cackling loudly, swallows twitter, unmistakable
V-shaped flocks.
Under the black sky, on Hallowe'en,
ghoulish masks,
scary costumes, haunted houses, yummy sweets,
children roam the streets.
Mouth-watering berries, as tender as chicken
birds feast
on juicy brambles,
thorny, swaying branches, plunge
into your skin.
Noisy echoes fill the sky, roaring flames,
Whistling
rockets, red, blue, green, light up the night.

Blair Johnstone (10)
Kennoway Primary & Community School

Autumn

A utumn leaves rustle in the breeze,
an icy wind blasts the leaves off the trees,

U nder the water, scaly, slippery creatures lurk,
from river to waterfall they leap,
struggling to get over, to get over, the misty water,
they travel swiftly to spawn,

T he swallow has a combed crest,
when it leaves its nest,
it flutters as gracefully as a ballet dancer,

U nder the swaying branches lie crispy, golden leaves,
with dog-eared ends, spots, crunchy, like stamping
in a blanket of snow,

M isty fog, like smoke surrounding us,
a damp haze of mini-droplets,
too light to fall to the ground,

N ovember the 5th, huge rockets fill the night sky,
exploding with a blaze of coloured stars,
ear-splitting Catherine wheels spin
in a circle of sparks,
fiery, sparkling, blazing bonfire.

Joshua Smith (10)
Kennoway Primary & Community School

Autumn

Autumn, the leaves, crispy, brittle, bright and beautiful.
Falls easily as a bird coming to land.
On the golden brown landscapes.

Umbrellas shining out in the rain.
Keeping us all pleasant and dry.
Where would we be without an umbrella?

The winds, gusty, strong, powerful, a tornado.
Taking out anything that meets the eye.
Gently shaking the clothes on the washing line.

Under the rocking trees lies the forest floor.
Crispy leaves, tiny hedgehogs, beautiful birds.
Leaves as yellow as the sun, leaves as red as fire.

Migration, it's time for the birds to go.
Preparing in massive flocks.
Seeking the beaming sunlight.

Not enough sun, out come the woolly hats
To keep us fine and cosy.
People trembling in the street.
Freezing in the frosty air.

Craig Donnelly (10)
Kennoway Primary & Community School

Remembrance

R emember all the people who got killed for our freedom.

E vil enemies bombed our land.

M emories will be with us forever. All that's gone will be forever.

E nemies killed our lovers. We will still love them from the land above us.

M ental illness troubled our soldiers and fear filled their minds.

B rave soldiers fought for our land.

R eturning back home injured from the war.

A ngry soldiers lost their friends.

N asty smells filled the air.

C asualties lying all around on the ground.

E very day we will remember those who died in the war.

Thomas Fraser (11)
Kennoway Primary & Community School

Remembrance

R emember all of the people who died for our peace and freedom.

E ven those who came back alive couldn't replace that empty space left in people's hearts.

M oping miserably about, not knowing what to do next, thinking your life is over.

E nemies fighting, throwing punches, blood flying everywhere, gangs charging.

M ilitary leaders conjuring plans, standing in a corner protected by soldiers.

B attleships covering the sea, bombs flying, blowing up other ships.

R aging soldiers rushing and dodging, desperately avoiding bombs.

A drenalin pumping through the bodies of many anxious soldiers.

N avigation systems on full alert, sneaking by the ships.

C old, dark trenches, full of boys crying for their mothers.

E mpty minds, wandering about, trying to get home, forgetting who they are.

Megan Penny (11)
Kennoway Primary & Community School

Remembrance

R ifles shooting, killing innocent soldiers.

E veryone dreading gas attacks and exploding bombs.

M en as young as sixteen receiving horrible letters telling them to report for duty.

E motional families crying to be reunited with their dads and brothers.

M ental and physical scars could never be mended.

B ombing in the city, destroying houses and killing people.

R oaring engines of tanks crashing their way into battle.

A irforces buzzing around, dropping bombs over the enemy.

N ever forgiven are the Nazis or Hitler.

C hemical gases filling lungs of brave soldiers and innocents.

E veryone who died is gone but not forgotten.

Nicole Fortune (11)
Kennoway Primary & Community School

Remembrance

R emember those soldiers who gave up their lives, families and friends to give us freedom and peace to live.

E veryone suffering from strong gases, large bombs and severe injuries.

M emories of soldiers forgotten and lost, the smells and images left behind from the war.

E nemies attacking and killing people for no reason.

M ental illnesses affected many involved.

B rave soldiers sent off to fight, one man who put many lives at risk.

R ed blood from the wounded and dead, soaked up by a bed of poppies.

A ll ammunition used twenty-four hours a day.

N ever ever will we want this to happen again, a terrible time to live.

C asualties lie there dying a slow, painful death.

E ndless deaths for those who were innocent.

Casey Galloway (11)
Kennoway Primary & Community School

Remembrance

R emember the soldiers who fought for our country.

E motions destroyed, families whose husbands and sons were fighting.

M emories of the people who had courage to go and fight.

E veryone dreading the bombs and gas attacks.

M emorial services thank the soldiers who fought for their own country.

B ravery shown by the terrified soldiers.

R emember they put their country before themselves.

A tomic bombs dropped destroyed houses and memories and pictures.

N ever forgotten them because of what they have done for us.

C hristmas without some of the family.

E mpty inside as you think back to the good days you had.

Louise Gilmour (11)
Kennoway Primary & Community School

Remembrance

R unning away from soldiers and bullets.

E nemies attacking, people fleeing for safety.

M emorial service, people old and young come to remember the past.

E nclosed and wounded, dead bodies everywhere.

M emories for those who died.

B rave soldiers charging along.

R emember those who put their country before themselves.

A ngry soldiers.

N asty smells linger for years.

C hildren screaming, mums crying.

E very year we will remember those who died.

Aaron Wilson (11)
Kennoway Primary & Community School

Remembrance

R ed is the colour of the poppies in the poppy field, where the men lay dead.

E xhausted soldiers willing helplessly for war to come to an end.

M ournful relatives concerned, waiting for news of their beloved.

E ndless painful deaths of talented, adored British soldiers.

M en and young boys leaving families, friends, children and girlfriends behind.

B ringing pride back to Britain for our lifestyles and design.

R eturning soldiers, ever so guilty for the loss of close friends.

A bused soldiers sitting, lonely, in the cold, dark trenches, worrying about their families.

N o chance to fight against war, no chance for life another day.

C elebrating the freedom and peace from this day on.

E mpty inside as we remember those who fought for our country.

Ashley Farmer (11)
Kennoway Primary & Community School

Zebra

On the dusty African road,
A black and white crossing,
Plods about the grassland,
And she hee-haws like a donkey.
Then I saw her legs,
They are small, like bamboo,
She behaves like a small horse,
Her fur is like a chequered flag.

Adam Terris (11)
Kinglassie Primary School

Duck

Its beak is two slippers joined at the heel,
Quack, quack.
Swims like a paddle steamer,
Swish, swash.
Doggy-paddling feet,
Flip-flap.
Feathers all over like a boa,
Tickle, tickle.

There he goes,
Quack, quack.
Swish-swash,
Flip flap,
Tickle, tickle.

Melanie Burns (11)
Kinglassie Primary School

Seal

A fat raindrop shape,
With velvety fur,
As shy as a mouse,
In the sea it's a blur.

With deep, black hole eyes,
And an innocent face,
It swims in the sea,
With loads of space.

Abbie Hutchison (11)
Kinglassie Primary School

Pig

A Christmas pudding shape,
With pink sandpaper skin,
A pepper-pot nose,
And a knobbly chin.

It's very clever and very lazy,
With baby legs and pointy ears,
A springy tail that swings so gently,
And little eyes that fill with tears.

Danielle Gaughan (11)
Kinglassie Primary School

A Snake

As long as rope, he slithers along the sand
His scaly tiles making shapes on the ground
He is fast like a rocket, his teeth are sharp as knives
His temper is terrible, like a tiger at night
He is bright as the sun
And he is camouflaged like a zebra.

Chloe Taylor (10)
Kinglassie Primary School

Gorilla

She was there looking at me,
With her hook arms up in the tree,
Her face as a moon in the sky,
Legs like trees to walk,
Her body as a chair to sit,
She came down from the tree.

Gemma Fleming (11)
Kinglassie Primary School

The Spell

Round and round the potion goes.
Adding some of a dead frog's toes.
The brain of a mouse and tongue of a cat.
The eye of a toad and nose of a bat.

Ear of a human, heart of a pig.
Skin of a snake and hair from a wig.
For a charm of powerful troubles.
That's the way the potion bubbles.

John Naylor (11)
Kinglassie Primary School

The Dolphin

Look at the dolphin,
It prowls,
Roams,
Swoops,
Flees,
Races,
Dives,
And even dashes through the warm
Sparkly waters of the Caribbean.

I, the dolphin, have a long, black nose,
A silky body.

I eat other fish,
Small sea creatures, that roam around in
The warm, sparkly waters of the Caribbean.

I love to swim and be free,
So please leave me.

Ashleigh Thomson (11)
Ladybank Primary School

Sea Horse

Slippy, golden, shy sea horse,
Strong, sandy, stumpy ones,
Slip softly behind the coral.
Shy babies as well,
Sleek, shiny as the water reflects,
Simple greenish ones.

Struggling sea horse emerges from the coral,
Glides smoothly through the sea,
Sunlit habitat.
Coral is all it is
Silly sea horse sleeping on a rock.

Catriona Duncan (11)
Ladybank Primary School

Wolf

Mine is the howl that chills the night,
Mine is the fur that gleams in the light.
I slink through the wood as
Guns that shouldn't be
Are firing at me.

You with dogs and horses and men,
Me with my pack and trees for hiding.
You hunt with only *your* permission,
I live with permission from Mother Nature herself.
But guns that shouldn't be
Are still firing at me.

Ceri Griffiths (11)
Ladybank Primary School

A Wolf's Life

Lean body with a fur coat
Razor-sharp claws
Strong legs
With determined jaws.
Quietly hunting for a meal
Hoping to get something every day
Getting ready to pounce on its prey.
Quietly moving when it's near rabbits
Whoosh it went.
Roar it says
Going back to its hole.
He feels he has become a hunting king
Going into the blackness of his home.
Until the next day he would say
What a hard day!

Andrew Anderson (10)
Ladybank Primary School

The Grizzly Bear

Back and forward people stare,
Wow! look at that huge, brown grizzly bear,
I'm kept in a cage and that's not fair,
I want to be free in the forests out there.

Come near my cage then be aware,
For I am the huge, brown grizzly bear,
Don't just stare, take care
Come near my lair, go on if you *dare!*

Callum Murray (11)
Ladybank Primary School

Red Raw Fox

Red raw fox,
White as snow,
Tip to its tail,
Pricked up ears,
Dark as night.

Slippery sly fox,
Quickly out-foxes,
Out-classing speeds,
Pitter-patter of its paws,
Just like raindrops,
Foxy fly fantastic
Fox!

Jack Wright (11)
Ladybank Primary School

Tiger

I am a tiger,
Beautiful creature,
Golden coat with a stripy feature.

I silently creep,
Then I suddenly leap,
Lean and mean,
With a shiny sheen.

I have a loud roar,
But now life's a bore,
I look at the door,
And realise I can't run anymore.

Russell Hope (11)
Ladybank Primary School

Lion

In the forest of North Africa,
Taking big heavy strides,
As you hear the deep roaring sound,
Through the head of his bushy mane,
With his long sharp claws.
Ready to pounce on his prey,
To have a feast
With sharp, golden teeth
And the colour goes with its rough hair,
'I am a big creature and I am proud.'

Amy Chalmers (11)
Ladybank Primary School

Fox

When I hunt,
I prowl,
I stalk,
I growl,
Glinting by the light of the moon.
I crouch,
I stare,
I sniff,
I glare,
You'll be in my stomach soon.

But when hunted,
I tear,
I dash,
I hare.
Bounding, not looking back.
I pant,
I pine,
I howl,
I whine,
A gunshot behind me and . . .
Black!

Victoria Robertson (11)
Ladybank Primary School

Shetland Pony

Bushy tail, tangled mane,
Dark as nightfall its shaggy coat,
This lovely, cute creature
With such short legs.
Its bouncy canter and wild trot.
How can it do it, just like that?

Out in the field, eating luscious grass,
It feels so free, galloping about.
While in its stable stuck with hay
It feels so down nearly every day.
Not being able to canter about
So sad and hurt, it can't get out.
It thinks about when it lived in the Highlands,
Those lovely times it had with its friends.

Annabel Laura Baker (11)
Ladybank Primary School

Poultry

My kicking clucking cockerel,
Struts around his run.
Golden bronze
Peacock blue,
Shiny black
Many battles fought and won.

My kicking clucking cockerel,
He does love eating bugs,
Golden wheat,
Dark brown oats.
All scattered round his run,
He always tugs at worms.

Luke Crawford (11)
Ladybank Primary School

The Wolf

I'm a wolf,
I live in a zoo.
I should be able to leap and creep like you,
Long ago I lived in the wild,
I was free like I should be.

Look at me, the wolf,
I'm loud,
I'm proud,
But . . .
I'm surrounded by a crowd.

I'm in a zoo
It's cruel
It should be against the rules.

I'm in a zoo,
I'm all on my own.
I used to run free,
Run with the wolves
But . . .
I can't!

Lindsay McDiarmid (11)
Ladybank Primary School

Why?

Why do I have to try?
Why does the wind blow?
Why do babies cry?
Why do flowers grow?

Why is water cold?
Why do birds fly?
Why are eggs bold?
Why is there a sky?

Why can't we fold?
Why do we have to buy?
Why do people get told?
Why do I have a school tie?

Megan Dick (9)
Lochgelly South Primary School

Why?

Why do babies cry?
Why are some people shy?
Why do birds fly?
Why do we have ears?

Why are people afraid of mice?
Why do we talk?
Why do we roll the dice?
Why do I have thoughts?

Why do I spy?
Why does the teacher use chalk?
Why do we have friends?

Why am I nine?
Why do I have a family?
Why am I not fine?
Why do I have eyes?

Megan Waterson (9)
Lochgelly South Primary School

Why?

Why do we go to school?
Why is the sky blue?
Why is the country so big?
Why do cows go moo?

Why do people die?
Why are seas so big?
Why do people eat pies?
Why do people wear wigs?

Why do we have cars?
Why do people have jobs?
Why do we live in houses?
Why do doors have knobs?

Lauren Adams (9)
Lochgelly South Primary School

My Favourite Colour

Red is . . .
For the team Man Utd.
The planet Mars which floats in space,
And the red Ferrari that is fast and furious
And the red, burning sun.

Red is . . .
For the tasty jam,
The red bright blood,
And the Pepsi Max roller coaster
And the red paint.

Red is . . .
For Arsenal, the football team.
England's cross on their flag
And paper that you draw on
And a carpet which people walk on.

Lewis Hamill (9)
Lochgelly South Primary School

My Favourite Colour

Green is . . .
True green grass in the summer days
P5 smilies tell us that the teacher's happy
Light green apples, crunchy and ripe
Superstar cards. Have you worked well?

Green is . . .
Truly bright hair for fancy dress parties,
Tasty fruity lollies, yum-yum
Fluorescent green for a bright picture,
Leaves that change colour in the autumn days.

Green is . . .
Crocodiles so scary in the muddy swamps
Sponges that we use to keep us clean,
The chalk that the teacher uses to write
On the blackboard.
The text books that we use to work out of.

Shannen Hunter (9)
Lochgelly South Primary School

Why?

Why do birds have to fly?
Why does the sun have to shine?
Why do people have to die?
Why is there a line?

Why do people play games?
Why do people have to scare?
Why do we live in houses?
Why do people have hair?

Why do we have doors and windows?
Why do we have water in the sea?
Why do we have to go to school?
Why do I have blood in me?

Amy Fong (9)
Lochgelly South Primary School

My Favourite Colour

Red is . . .
A soft cuddly teddy
A tasty, juicy strawberry
A horrible slimy pot of paint
A red rose that smells nice.

Red is . . .
A balloon that is fun to play with
A car that you can travel in to go on holiday,
A sunset that you can see in summer
A red ball that you can play with.

Red is . . .
An easy SHM 3 textbook
A folder to keep paper in,
A rose to put in your garden
A light to help you see.

Amy Kearns (9)
Lochgelly South Primary School

Why?

Why are we at school?
Why am I small?
Why are there books?
Why is my family so tall?

Why are there so many people?
Why are there too many mice?
Why are there flowers?
Why is my teacher so nice?

Why are there twins?
Why are some people so bad?
Why do I have fingers?
Why are some people so sad?

Kirsty Young (9)
Lochgelly South Primary School

My Favourite Colour

Brown is . . .
Some sizzling sausages I have for dinner
The glowing eyes that you can see with at night,
The sweet chocolate that gives me energy
A cowboy's hat that keeps his head warm.

Brown is . . .
A stretchy piece of string that stretches
Around a pole
A big brown pencil that I write with
A huge smooth piece of wood
The scrumptious burger that is crispy.

Brown is . . .
A huge wall that keeps us in school
A big fence that goes around the house
A small hamster that crawls about the house
The hair you have on your head.

James Bernard (9)
Lochgelly South Primary School

My Favourite Colour

Orange is . . .
Bright shining sun in the day
Giant orange stars in the midnight sky
Fizzy bubbly Irn Bru
Great roasting, burning fires.

Orange is . . .
Juicy fruity chunks of orange
Jelly - bright orange pens
The cool orange pencil
Warm coloured paper.

Orange is . . .
A nice evening sky
A long dark orange rug
Big, nice, bright carpet
Hungry, fast, stripy tiger.

Kyle Brockie (9)
Lochgelly South Primary School

Shopping

S ensational fashion all in the mind,
H ot boys looking at my friends and me,
O pening doors to the dressing chamber,
P arty girl coming through.
P eople staring at all my shopping bags
I ncoming gorgeous gal,
N o one's able to stop me,
G lam nail varnish on my fingertips.

Becci Douglass (11)
Lynburn Primary School

The Shadowman

It turns to 9.30pm
It's time to go to bed.
I give everyone a kiss,
I know the shadowman's there.

I thump up the stairs,
To let him know I'm coming.
I reach the top and make one last thud,
I go into the bathroom and brush my teeth.

Smack! I open the door, I push it against the wall
To squash his face.
Click! I turn the light on
I see him on my bed.

'No one sleeps in my bed,' I say,
Then I jump on the bed until he's gone.
Oh no, I forgot to turn the light off and shut the door.

I jump down and I jump to the light
So I can stand on his head.
I turn the light off and whack the door shut.

That teaches him for living in my room,
'You can sleep outside my bedroom tonight.'

Jade Kehoe (11)
Lynburn Primary School

The Snow Blizzard

Once upon a rhyme there was a
snow blizzard who loved to sing
and one day he made up a singing
rhyme, he wanted to sing
the snow blizzard who loves to sing.

The snow blizzard who wanted
to sing he made something
he could sing and rhyme
and he would have enough time
the snow blizzard who loved to sing.

The snow blizzard who told his
friends he can sing and rhyme the
snow blizzard got angry and then
did his favourite thing, sing and rhyme
the snow blizzard who loved to sing.

The snow blizzard, the fierce storm
of wind and snow, started to blow
he decided he should go but
thought no and stayed to sing
the snow blizzard who loved to sing.

The snow blizzard who sung again
wrote another singing rhyme but
got stuck and couldn't think of
another singing rhyme and then had some slime
the snow blizzard who loved to sing.

The snow was like a spinning
washing machine of fur, the snow
blizzard was full of rhymes and
he likes to sing and rhyme
the snow blizzard who loved to sing.

Ewan Paterson (11)
Lynburn Primary School

The Crying Child

It was as black as night,
When I heard the child crying on the moors,
The crying became clearer as I walked closer,
Suddenly I saw a child crying her eyes out.

It was as black as night
When I heard the child crying on the moors.
I asked her what's wrong,
'I've lost my mum,' said she.

It was as black as night,
When I heard the child crying on the moors.
I looked around the misty sky but could not see
All was lost by the dark skies.

It was as black as night
When I heard the child crying on the moors.
Suddenly all went quiet as I saw a figure
But the figure would not come closer.

It was as black as night,
When I heard the child crying on the moors.
The figure came closer to reveal the child's mother,
Suddenly all went light!

Stuart Taylor (11)
Lynburn Primary School

Death's Feast

A life is a terrible thing to waste,
Death lives for that taste.
The menacing cries of banshees destroying brittle bones.
The brick hard thuds of bullies,
The vile thoughts of death.
The deep yellow eyes of cats.
The blinding light at the end of the tunnel,
The terrible final scene, brutal.
The distraught family members,
A life is a terrible thing to waste.
Death lives for that taste.
The destruction of mankind,
Man buried six feet under.
Babies being burned in Hell,
Children being crucified by clowns.
Woman wiped from the face of the Earth.
Families being flame-grilled,
Dogs being destroyed,
Cats caged and burned,
A life is a terrible thing to waste,
Death lives for that taste.

Craig Forbes (11)
Lynburn Primary School

Once Upon A Dream

Fairy tales are ones of old or so I'm told,
But please folks, if I may be so bold as to tell you my story today.
You won't regret it, as my friend Silky, she has always had a technique
to capture your imagination for more than just a week.
Though, if you don't believe in such as fairies, elves and the like,
this true tale may come as a shock, but please refrain from leaving,
as you soon will be believing.

There once was a fabulously funky fairy, her name was Silky,
With a complexion as white and milky as a lily, floating on a
serene pond.
She was the Queen of Dreams.
Her quarters were in Aurora Castle, sheltering amongst the
shady green leaves of an oak.
Waiting until dawn to give all extremely sweet dreams.

The only thing that ever faltered her, was good and evil,
right and wrong.
Silky thought evil should be punished and good - rewarded,
But she had no power over the god's immoral choices.
So foolishly she protested which was like a red rag to a bull
but alas to no avail,
Silky was put to death by Atria, the Goddess of Evil,
Silky's most hated rival.
As she was put to death, everyone mourned, not only for Silky,
but for their precious sweet dreams.

Sarah-Jane Dale (11)
Lynburn Primary School

Once Upon A Rhyme

The sinful and sinister demon unwound on his scalding, heated home, burning away in the swarthy dark.
The offensive and unpleasant man called *Satan!* roars blatantly at the evil spirits lingering around him, squawking and grunting like eagles, for vengeance on the Devil.
He shrieked and bellowed, like an infuriated, shrilled troll, stampeding about like a rhino.
Satan bounds into the pool of immortality, mellowing away, still waiting to seek reprisals on the wicked spirits that observe the demon.

Satan waits for the evil spirits to arrive, so he can anguish and distress them like drudges.
The horrid Devil utters to the slaves to make an evil, cruel kingdom for him, the wicked one.
After the slaves are exhausted and harassed, they will get barely little time for tranquillity in the sordid, squalid, disastrous dungeons.
A little while later, the drudges get back to their fatigue-inducing work, pleading to stop but the Devil whips them as hard as he can and demands for them to work.
When the kingdom is made, the sinister cold-hearted man gets his guards to spring the slaves into the pit of death!

David J McManus (11)
Lynburn Primary School

White Blizzard

Once upon a rhyme, a white blizzard stormed through a barrier
of dark, black wind.
It spun like a boat on a stormy ocean of death,
It howled like bloodthirsty wolves who had found their prey.
The snow was as white as a Mammoth in the dark ages,
It covered the grass in a silk white cloak.
It brought snowflakes as light and thin as white wool,
It was as powerful as a forest full of mad, hungry,
death-killing bulls.
It was as fast as 1000 preying tigers, launching at their prey,
It was as quick-eyed as a fleet of calm, floating golden eagles.
It covered you in snow, like a gigantic death-killing wave.
It froze like a dark blue sea, frozen to the core.
It scared everything like a snow-breathing demon, as powerful
as 50,000 men.
It was as dangerous as a blood-thirsty, strong-witted beast,
Which is stronger than anything in this universe.
It was as hungry as five million lions, finding their daily feast.
It endured like fifty pieces of strong, powerful-witted iron,
steel, metal plates - joined together.
It got stronger, like a butterfly about to use its colourful, gigantic wings.
It stormed and rampaged, like mad, crazy rhinos.
Once upon a rhyme, a white blizzard stormed through a barrier of
dark, blue wind.

Darryl Simpson (11)
Lynburn Primary School

Weathermen

I meet the sun
That killed the rain,
Made the skies clear again.

No snow, no rain,
Little clouds disappear
Like sweets from the shop.

Lightning was furious
The rain had gone
And so had snow, revealing the sun.

Snow went east
Rain went west,
And sun stayed here, we like that best.

Lightning went north to look for snow,
Thunder went south to look for rain
But we never saw them ever again.

Clouds come and hide the sun
Locked like soft cuddly pillows
On a big bed in the sky.

The sun bursts through the cloud
Like a sword through a knight
Or a swimmer through water.

I meet the sun
That killed the rain
Made the skies clear again.

Michael Wilson (11)
Lynburn Primary School

Fairies

Tiptoe through the rose bushes
Like a tulip in the daisies
The diamonds in the rock
The sun in the sky
The sound of fluttering wings
The sense of safety

The whisper in the trees
The cries in the night
Like a carnival I see in the trees
Singing and dancing, with no cares
Light as air we breathe
Silent as sleep in the night.

Foxglove, tulip, daisy, daffodil
Dancing like only fairies can
Hand in hand, linked together,
Magic flowing from their hair
Then the men enjoy a dance
Pepper, thorn, oak, birch.

Alas they join together
United as they stand
Dance, dance
The love of dance
No more noise
They start to disappear.

Tiptoe through the rose bushes
Like a tulip in the daisies
The diamonds in the rock
The sun in the sky
The sound of fluttering wings
The sense of safety.

Samantha Fraser (11)
Lynburn Primary School

The Giant's Voice

It snored like a bang of thunder
And it spoke like a tiger's roar,
It screamed like a pack of bloodthirsty wolves
Chasing an animal in the dark.
The way a car makes its noise for a yawn
And it shakes the world with the way it walks.
It thumps its feet when it's angry,
It sounds like a rhinoceros charging
In the middle of the day.
Racing and racing forward, it's got what
It wants then it finally stops.
But then it sneezes and
Has blown the clouds away.
What a terrible thing to do!

Clare Gourlay (11)
Lynburn Primary School

Once Upon A Rhyme

Magic
Magic is like walking on thin air,
Magic is just like a new world.
You can wish for almost anything you want.
Magic is as soft as sleep,
I wish it was a kiddy-kid world,
Magic is a wonderful place.

Magic is as friendly as your own friend,
There's a magical place for every living thing.
Some magic can be dangerous and some magic is not.
Magic is like walking on thin air,
Magic is just like a new world.
You can wish for almost anything you want.

Erin McRae (11)
Lynburn Primary School

Happiness

Happiness is a scorching yellow
Happiness tastes like an ice cream
Happiness smells like roast turkey
Happiness sounds like victory
Happiness feels like winning the lottery
Happiness looks like Henrik Larsson,
Scoring a goal.

Sam Gibson (11)
Lynburn Primary School

Once Upon A Waterfall

Once there was a waterfall,
It was far into the woods
It sings to the animals
Falling off the rock,
It dances like a ballerina sweetly on the waterfall
The sun shines on it, like a golden star.

The birds sing to her as she sings to them
She sings when she's sleeping,
She sings all day long as softly as she can,
She laughs so amusingly
When she sings
As the animals listen to her.

She is so tall, she can see over the treetops
To see if anything is wrong,
She likes to look around
She falls asleep and the water is still
Rolling through the rocks,
It dances like a ballerina,
Sweetly on the waterfall.
The sun shines on it, like a golden star.

Kirsty Muir (11)
Lynburn Primary School

A Westie Called Kirsty

Kirsty is a Westie she likes to play all day,
She is very bubbly but that's okay.
She is very noisy till she gets her own way,
She's also very fluffy and she likes to play.
She likes to bite your nose,
She likes to tug at your clothes.
She likes to run, not sit and 'stay'
She likes to bite your toes,
So she can get away!

Gemma Day (11)
Lynburn Primary School

The Creepy Creature

In the deep dark cave
Lives a monstrous thing!
As it slithers and squirms
Through the deep dark drain.
Then you hear its *dreadful* cry
It's sure to pass you by
So start to hurry
And always worry.
When the creepy creature comes by,
When you see a bright light.
Don't get in a fright,
It's only the creature's eye!
But don't look away,
Unless you wish to die!
When the creepy creature comes by.

Leaha Robertson (11)
Lynburn Primary School

Ghosts And Ghouls

The ghostly ghouls came out tonight,
You had better watch out, they might give you a fright,
They have plenty of life,
As they walk about Fife.
Yes, oh yes! You had better watch out!

The ghostly ghouls come out tonight,
Yes I see their bright white light,
Come on out and play tonight,
We will give you joy and delight,
We must hurry back into the night.

We can't come out tonight,
As you see, it's still light.
But you just wait until tomorrow night,
You will be in for a terrible fright.
Oh you just wait until tomorrow night!

In the woods,
As dark as night.
As the ghosts and ghouls go past the trees,
The branches clutch,
The wind howls like a wolf at midnight.

In the cottage, in the dark, dark woods,
There the ghosts and ghouls rest.
There they sleep through the day, and
Then wake at 10.30pm
Now they begin to play!

Cheryl Cowan (11)
Lynburn Primary School

The Haunted House

The creepy old house
With its ghosts and ghouls,
It's as quiet as a mouse
And no swimming pools.

I went in
Went over creaky floors,
I tripped over the bin
Into self-shutting doors.

Screams I started to hear
Like a giant fruit bat.
I ran with fear
I fell and went splat!

I looked all around
Then I saw a ghost,
There were shivers in the grounds
It was burning like toast.

Screeching and screaming
I could hear with fear,
Around the table beaming
Were the ghosts, drinking beer.

The creepy old house
With its ghosts and ghouls,
It's always quiet as a mouse
And no swimming pools.

Neal Mullen (11)
Lynburn Primary School

Angels

Once upon a rhyme there was an angel
Who came from Wonderland,
The angels name was Sparkle
She was all very kind and grand.

Sparkle had a sister called Cinders
She thought she was bigger than them all,
But when it came to size
Cinders wasn't big, she was small.

Cinders was a mean and nasty person
Whilst Sparkle was very kind.
Sparkle was generous and had lots of manners
But Cinders didn't mind.

Cinders was as fast as a cheetah
When it came to racing and flying,
Sparkle was as slow as a tortoise
And because of this, she would end up crying.

Shy Sparkle, shining in the sky
Cruel Cinders hoping Sparkle would die,
Sparkle crying on a shining star
Cinders wondering if Sparkle is near or far.

Katie Westwater (11)
Lynburn Primary School

The Alien With Six Eyes

Hello, I am a six-eyed alien called Jock,
And I'm from the weirdest planet called Spock.
Spock is the greatest planet in the world
But sometimes I have to get my hair curled.
It's boring when I have no friends,
But I don't blame them, I don't have any trends.
This planet thinks I'm totally insane,
As it laughs while I'm eating a candy cane
My favourite food was delicious saucy beans,
But that was only when I was in my teens.
That was a long, long time ago,
About the time when I lost my big toe!

I have been on this planet since . . . oh I can't really remember!
I think it was about a hundred years ago, some time in December.
My favourite food now and will always be slime,
And I have liked slime for a very long time.
It is my birthday next week
But I won't have anyone to celebrate it with, because I am a geek!
I hardly know anything because I didn't go to school.
I wish so much I could have gone, it would have been awfully cool,
Going to another planet would be really great but I don't know where!
But on the other hand maybe not, lots of other people would
Stand and stare.

Shaun Philp (11)
Lynburn Primary School

Waterfall

She rushes down the mountain,
Hitting the rocks and splashing the flowers
She likes to crush canoes up in her waves
Her crashing, whooshing, crunching sounds
Are ear-splitting and deadly!

Nobody ever goes near her,
Apart from when they want to be killed.
They drop down into her deadly trap
She throws them with her waves
And they are never seen again.

I am the only one that understands her
I know she is a peaceful and placid place to be.
She would not harm people if they did not take her for granted,
They pollute her by covering her glistening water in black slimy oil
They throw rubbish in her and kill her water lilies and leaves
The reason I know her so well, is because that poor waterfall is me!

Jennifer Corke (11)
Lynburn Primary School

The Storm

A sunny day in Scotland.
People are screaming and shouting,
In the park, you can hear the birds singing.
You can hear the sun sizzling.

Oh no! the rain has started to spit down, drip-drop, splish-splash.
The rain gets heavier, bang, crash, boom;
Everyone puts up their umbrellas.
Tip tap, ping-pong, everyone goes inside,
Crash, strike goes the lightning

Then the wind comes, swish, whistle, moan.
Trees falling down, crack!
Branches hitting your window, bang!
Roof tiles falling off, thump!

Michael Boyle (11)
Lynburn Primary School

The Riddle

I am authoritative
I am as powerful as a giant wave
I weigh 180kg
I can eat you whole
I am as long as a limousine
Don't come near me or else!
I am very slimy
I shed my skin
What am I?
Who am I?

Neil Davidson (11)
Lynburn Primary School

Snow

Once there was a cloud,
Whose best friend was the snow.
They played together and talked together,
Through the winter's night.
The snow was very sparkly,
Even fluffy too.
It made the air chilly
Everyone loved the snow.
It always made them laugh,
They played on their sledges,
On the icy hills.
It was always very happy.
Especially soft and huggable.
So one day, it went away
But said, 'It's okay, I'll be back to play!'

Nicola Campbell (11)
Lynburn Primary School

Falling Out

She started it, she kicked me in the leg,
But of course she thinks I started it,
She says I punched her in the nose!

There would have been a fight,
But the teacher caught us.
'Blah! Blah! Make up,' says the teacher.

I didn't want to make up at the time, but now I do,
I want to go and talk to her but I've gone all shy.
She's got her friends and I've got mine.

My dad says he didn't like her anyway,
He says I'm better off with my new friends.
Maybe he's right, but I don't want him to be.

I had to work with her and she hardly said anything,
I miss when we used to write letters to each other
Across the classroom,
And have a right good laugh.

Naiomi Keay (11)
Lynburn Primary School

Rat City

Deep down in the sewers, lies rat city,
You will never ever find it, because it is hidden,
As the sun rises, they tuck into their beds
The howl of the wolves, waken them as the moon shines.

Rats are busy making homes,
You might even find one in the pipes.
The blue siren is glowing on and off,
That means the rain is coming.

All the rats scurry into their homes and close their doors,
Rats are born and rats are passing away,
But deep down in the sewers -
Lies a wonderful place.

Allyson Mullen (11)
Lynburn Primary School

The Haunted Mine

Anyone who enters my haunted mine,
I will cover them in my darkness,
I will make you taste my slime.

I will find you,
There's nowhere to go,
Show your face and I will eat you whole.

I'll make you scream in the night,
I'll gave you the chance to show your face,
Now I'm going to bite you!

Sean Jordan (11)
Lynburn Primary School

Idioms

My mum said
I was the talk of the Devil
(But I'm not a Devil).

My teacher said
I drove her round the bend.
(But I smashed my car right up).

My sister said
I was butter fingers
(So I licked it all off).

My brother said
It's no use crying over spilt milk
(But all the milk was in my tea).

My cousin said
He caught me red-handed.
(But my hand is peach).

My auntie said
I was to suffer a curtain lecture.
(But my curtains don't speak)!

Damien Scott (11)
Lynburn Primary School

The Football That Has Its Own Mind

He goes for the shot,
It's over the keeper.
What! It's stopped?
There's something up here!

Larsson for the head,
But the ball's moved.
It's going straight to Douglas
What! It's in the net!

Miller is going for the ball
It's coming straight to him.
This can't be happening,
The ball's chasing him.

Right Petrov's got the ball
He goes for the shot.
It's on the line but it's moved back
This football's got a mind of its own!

Callum Moran (11)
Lynburn Primary School

The Monster

The monster under my bed is
Very minuscule to get under my bed
He is wee bit alarming.
He is blue with green spots,
He is called Charlie,
He has razor teeth.
He has humongous muscles,
He likes dark places,
He has no shadow,
He hates vast places.
He is very humorous,
He comes out at night to tell jokes.
He is as strong as an ox,
But he is my best friend.

Craig Robert Dearie (11)
Lynburn Primary School

Kala The Horse

There was once a horse
Her name was Kala
Everybody loved her.

Her tail went swish and swoosh
Brown eyes glittering
Like a torch beam.

She was very cuddly
And she liked to snuggle in
Her fur was very shiny,
She also liked it being brushed.

All she ever did was neigh, neigh, neigh!
Her chestnut coat was also very clean
And she liked to get a bath.

She also liked to run
But she also liked to play,
When the children went to see her,
She chased them all away.

Hayley Smith (11)
Lynburn Primary School

My Dog Dylan

D ylan was a cheerful dog
Y ou would love his wagging tail, back and forth it went
L aying in the sunlight, Dylan loved to do
A ball Dylan used to hit with his head, through the fields and gardens
N ow that he's dead. I miss him so much.
    Dylan I loved you.

Craig Morgan (11)
Newburgh Primary School

My Family

My mum is definitely great!
She goes to yoga and is a great mate!

My dad is definitely great!
He goes to golf and is a great mate!

My sister is definitely great!
She goes to Brownies and is a great mate!

When it comes to me . . .
My family say that I'm a pest
But that doesn't change the way
I'm loved!

Denise Claire Corcoran (11)
Newburgh Primary School

Her!

Her!
Her eyes are like golf balls
Her!
Her hair is like spaghetti
Her!
Her nose is like a blow-up balloon
Her!
Her breath smells like a garbage can
Her!
Her ears are like blowing flames
Her!
Her neck is like a giraffe
Her!
Her arms are like twigs
Her!
Her fingers are like walking sticks
Her!
Her feet are like bananas
Her!
Her bum sticks out like Mount Everest.

Steven May (11)
Newburgh Primary School

My Brother

My friends think he's cute
He can sometimes be a brute
Invading my space
Oh what a disgrace
My things get broken
I am outspoken
He is a pest
Doesn't live in a nest
My brother.

Tendai Calley (11)
Newburgh Primary School

My Hamster

I have a hamster called Crystle,
Who drinks like a water pistol,
Although she is blind,
She doesn't mind,
For food she can find,
And water is always at hand!

If I take her to the vet,
I won't have a pet!
She'll be put to sleep
And I'd like to keep
My hamster with me!

I know she's okay
For a day she lay
And then up she got
And she played a lot.

Hailey Dalrymple (11)
Newburgh Primary School

Monsters

Monsters are scary
Monsters are hairy
Monsters are big

Monsters have big teeth
Monsters need a leash
Monsters have jaws
Monsters have paws
Which have sharp claws.

Stuart Allen (11)
Newburgh Primary School

A Holiday

A summer holiday

A summer holiday
A trip away

A summer holiday
A trip away
Trips to the beach

A summer holiday
A trip away
Trips to the beach
Lots of ice cream and lollies

A summer holiday
A trip away
Trips to the beach
Lots of ice cream and lollies
And what great fun!

Michael Simpson (11)
Newburgh Primary School

My Sister

My sister gets on my nerves,
She takes all my things and never gives them back.
When my friends come round, she bugs me until I play with her,
In the morning, I'm watching TV until my sister bites and kicks me.
My little sister gets on my nerves, but I don't know where I would be
Without her.

Kirsty Wilkie (11)
Newburgh Primary School

Why I Love Animals

I love animals because they need to be loved
Some are cuddly and full of fun
Some can be bad and that makes me sad.
Some animals are funny in the bath
And sometimes can be silly and daft.
Some animals can run fast and some are slow
But it doesn't matter if they win or come last.
Horses can run fast but they also can come last.
Cats are funny and crazy but are also very lazy,
Dogs can bark a lot at night but when it becomes bright,
They like to give you a fright by being suddenly quiet.
Rabbits can be small or big, but they love to dig.
A sheep can jump and they also can leap.

Stacey Dick (11)
Pitcoudie Primary School

Football

What a game played by many
Beckham, Davids and Mackilvenny
Played by the young
Played by the old
Played by the brave and the bold.
Up the middle
Up the wing
Cross the ball and have a ping!
Can you believe
We love it so much?
Get the ball and take a 'touch'.
It could be you
It could be me
Keep on training and wait and see.
On the park
Or in the street,
Let's keep the ball at our feet.
Don't be sad
Don't be snappy
Taking part will make you happy
Don't cheat and don't abuse
You will be the one to lose.
Keep it clean
Keep it nice
Just play the game and take my advice.

Keelan Breeze (10)
Pitcoudie Primary School

My Friend

Buttons, Buttons, all so sweet and so nice,
Stays in the kitchen because it's too cold outside.
My best friend isn't at school but at home, all nice and warm.
When I get home I let him run round and round like a roundabout.
Whenever I'm sad Buttons makes me feel happy by licking my hand.
He listens to you and answers by nodding his head or turning away.
He likes going behind the TV and knows not to bite the cables.
I feel like the luckiest girl in the world because I have a pet rabbit.

Ashleigh Cruickshank (11)
Pitcoudie Primary School

My Pet

I have a rabbit called Finlay
Who's a very special pet
He's cared for and looked after
And always checked by the vet.

I have a rabbit called Finlay
Who lives in a hutch full of hay
It's warm and clean and cosy
It helps keep the cold at bay.

I have a rabbit called Finlay
Who likes to run in the sun
He hops and skips and jumps
And always seems to have fun.

I have a rabbit called Finlay
Who eats apples and corn and beans
He's happy and healthy
And always eats up his greens.

I have a rabbit called Finlay
His colour is grey and white
He is very special to me
And I love him day and night.

Murray Anderson (10)
Pitcoudie Primary School

Pitcoudie Pitcoudie

Pitcoudie, Pitcoudie
It's great if you're moody
Cos when you wake up
It cheers you up cos you know
It's time to go to Pitcoudie

Pitcoudie, Pitcoudie
We're on our way, we won't be late
We cannot wait, the bell will go
The teachers will know that we'll be in
To make a din at Pitcoudie

Pitcoudie, Pitcoudie
It's time to learn
While the teachers earn
And the janitor doesn't rest
Cos he knows we're the best
Pitcoudie

Pitcoudie, Pitcoudie
The girls and boys
Have played with the toys
And their coats are
On the hooks
Their noses are stuck in books
And if they're in luck, they will soon get some tuck.

Pitcoudie, Pitcoudie
In the afternoon
Before we say goodbye
You'll hear the teachers sigh
And then they'll say, 'Bye! Bye!'

Hannah Bell (11)
Pitcoudie Primary School

The Lady From Govan

There was a young lady from Govan
Who bought a new microwave oven,
When asked what it cost,
Her memory she lost
And was rushed right away to the Southern.

When she got there
Her soul she did bare,
To the nurse who was there.

'Oh what a cost,
No wonder you lost,
Your memory today,' said Nurse Halliday.

'My lady be careful,
Do not be fearful,
To look at these prices
And not cause a crisis!

Your place is in Govan,
And not in the Southern.
So what I suggest
Is you go home and rest
And do your best
To heed this test of bargain shopping.'

Michael Brady (11)
Pitcoudie Primary School

Love Is . . .

Love is a feeling in everyone
Love is a passion in everyone,
Love is a feeling so, so great,
Love is the opposite of hate.
Love is a shining light.
When you're in love you do not fight,
Love is in everyone,
Love is a special feeling,
That everyone has.
Love is in everyone!

Greg Patrick (11)
Pitcoudie Primary School

My Life

When I was two
I lost my shoe,
When I was three
I hurt my knee.
But then I turned four,
And I just wanted more.
It was great being five
All I did was jive,
At six I played with sticks.
Being seven, was just Heaven.
When I was eight
I felt just great,
At nine I went to bed at nine.
Being ten I got a new pen,
Now I'm eleven
I might go to Devon.

Michael Murray (11)
Pitcoudie Primary School

Fashion

I love fashion
I love clothes
I love the way models strike their pose.

I love designer shops
Which sell Burberry tops.

Calvin Klein
Fcuk
I wear La Senza, every day.

Gucci, Versace
Stella McCartney
What more could a girl ask for?
How about Christian Dior?
Burberry touch, Gucci Rush
Oh, it all smells so lush.

I love fashion
I love clothes
Why can't I be a model and strike a pose!

Rachel Robertson (11)
Pitcoudie Primary School

Football

Football is the best game in the world
It is better than anything else,
Nothing can beat it, it's just so great,
I love hitting the net and making it break.
I am a striker up front,
I score loads of goals with a punt.
It's great to play, I love to watch it too
Especially when Scotland's winning by two!

Connor Robertson (11)
Pitcoudie Primary School

My Cousin Rachel

I have a little cousin aged two
Who's a friendly little girl
Her eyes are blue,
Her hair is fair
And has a little curl.
She comes to visit every week
And I take her for a walk.
We play some games and watch TV
I love to hear her talk
She watches Barney every day,
I sometimes watch it with her.
She likes to play with her teddy bears
But she loves me like her brother.

Stewart Wright (11)
Pitcoudie Primary School

My Cat

She's long and thin, a striped cat
She's always really been like that
Always running and wants to play
I think she's like that every day
She sleeps all day and plays all night
She hides behind the curtains and gives me a fright
She scratches the couch and makes my mum shout
And I hear her say, 'Get that cat out!'
She sits in the bath and drinks from the tap.
Yes, that's Em, my favourite cat.

Beth Goodall (10)
Pitcoudie Primary School

Animals

'Pussy cat, pussy cat,
        What have you done?'
'I've eaten a rat, out in the sun.'

'Slithery snake, slithery snake
        What have you seen?'
'I've been to see a big machine.'

'Brave bear, brave bear
        Where have you been?'
'I've been to the palace to see the Queen.'

'Fantastic fox, fantastic fox
        What have you eaten?'
'I've eaten a nice round juicy ferret.'
Slurp! Slurp! Slurp!

Vanessa Walker (10)
Pitcoudie Primary School

Tornadoes

Tornadoes are very strong
The effect lasts very long
It destroys everything in its way
Then people will have to pay
Destruction, chaos and mess
Leaving everyone with less.

Jamie Dryburgh (11)
Pitcoudie Primary School

Wee Wifey

Gan ben the hoose
Says ma wee wifey
To ma braw wee bairn
That wiz drookit and
We'll gan doon the road
To the Kirk
We git in the Kirk
And ma wee wifey
Says to ma braw
Wee bairn wheesht
The noo ma braw wee
Bairn or you'll gan doon
The house yer sel.

Claire Morris (10)
Pitcoudie Primary School

Lookin Oot The Windie

Lookin oot the windie
Watchin the bairns climb the dike.
Dirty wee middins faces fue o' smiles
Nae fear o' fawin jist fue o' fun

When they get aulder they'll get like me
They'll watch their ain bairns and be foe
O happy memories.

Joanne Elkington (10)
Pitcoudie Primary School

My Hamster

I love my little hamster and
I know he loves me, I am not
too shy to go near him or to
talk to him to see, but my little
hamster must sleep during the
day and wake during the night,
so hush hamster, hush!

Linzi Forbes (10)
Pitcoudie Primary School

Candles

Lighting up the darkness,
Heating up the cold,
They come in different colours
Red and blue and gold.
Whilst they are burning slowly,
The flames they flicker bright,
I beg of you dear candle,
Please last me through the night.
Flickering in the darkness,
To guide us on our way;
To show us things that we would see
Upon the light of day.

They come in all shapes and sizes,
Some fat, some thin, some round.
To help those people praying
Who kneel upon the ground.

So quietly do you leave us,
We miss your little light,
But if we strike another match
You're back, you're shining bright!

Lucy Irvine (11)
Pitcoudie Primary School

A White Playground

I went to school on a cold winter's day,
When the bell rang we went out to play,
Snow started to fall down from the sky,
On the ground it was beginning to lie.

A snowflake landed on my cheek,
All around, the air was bleak,
Ferocious, chilly winds blew hard,
The playground looked like a Christmas card.

The branches of trees were covered in snow,
The green of the grass was no longer on show,
Icicles hung from the roof of the school,
And everyone seemed to think it was cool.

And on the way home at 3pm,
Children were starting to build some snowmen,
The older ones started a snowball fight,
One hit me in the face and I got such a fright.

But the very next morning the snow had all gone,
All I could see was a bright green lawn,
I was really quite sad, it'd all gone away,
But I'm sure it'll come back another day.

Christina Sharples (11)
Pitreavie Primary School

A Winter's Day

On a cold winter's day
Everyone is out to play
Everybody is playing with snow
Then a snowball fight starts, *oh no!*

It's freezing, it's bitter
Your teeth start to chatter
Some people pray for it to stay
Some people hope it goes away

Then you go to sleep one night
And you wake up to such a fright
The snow has gone, it's melted away
Parents shout, 'Hip, hip hooray!'

Peter Kelly (11)
Pitreavie Primary School

A Winter's Day

On a winter's day
All the birds fly away
They fly east
And we will sit down to a New Year's feast.

I love to play in the snow
Though I don't like to see it go
I play in the snow when it is deep
And I never ever get any sleep.

The best part of winter is when you finish school
Especially when it is really cool
The worst part is when it goes away
And there goes another winter's day.

Liam Miller (11)
Pitreavie Primary School

Snowfall

I went to bed late at night,
When I woke up, everything was all white,
The snow glistened and sparkled,
It was an amazing sight.

Children playing in the snow,
Rubbing their hands, their fingers aglow,
Sledging downhill, oh my gosh,
There goes Peter, Amanda and Josh.

Slipping and sliding, oh, what a pain,
Everybody falling again and again,
Here comes the teacher to help us out,
We're not injured, just mucking about.

There goes the bell,
We're all running in,
Slipping and sliding, just to get in.

Siobhan Paterson (11)
Pitreavie Primary School

A Scottish Winter

'Gi'es the dosh for the heatin'!'
As ma dad is always bleatin'

Oot in the garden, why did a' go?
It's crisp 'n siller wi' sleet and cauld
The air is still an' it's minus seven
But God bless the central heatin'!

A'm in the street
A'm nae fool
A'm going' to the heat
An' that's in the school

I've gotten hame as quick as a' could
But I've just been told . . . 'There's nae food!'
Sae a'm oot in the cauld and the snae once mare
Ta' gang to the shops, it's just nae fair!

Adam Reid (11)
Pitreavie Primary School

Wintry Week

One Monday in winter,
it was snowy, slippery and shivery,
the children went out to play,
almost every day,
sledging, skiing, and skating.

One Tuesday in winter,
it was freezing, frosty and foggy,
when again the children went out to play,
today they were sliding, singing and shouting,
before they went back to counting.

Then there was Wednesday, Thursday and Friday,
when all the snow was away,
not knowing what to do,
apart from polishing each shoe.

On Saturday and Sunday,
the days before Monday,
before they went back to school,
they all did their homework,
before they got more work,
and thought of the holidays, wouldn't you?

Catherine Madden (11)
Pitreavie Primary School

A Winter's Day

I woke up in the night,
The moon was really bright,
I didn't turn on the light,
To improve my sight.

Outside it was cold,
There were no people old,
It was freezing,
Everybody was sneezing.

It was snowing,
The snow was growing,
It was sleeting,
The sun was retreating.

Jack Martin-Jones (11)
Pitreavie Primary School

A Winter's Night

On a windy winter's night
The sky was dark and stars not bright
The wind was so cold and chilly
That going out with no coat would be silly
The streets were full of snow
It made people feel very low
The weather forecast was very bleak
They said there was going to be more sleet
With all this snow and rain
I wish I was going away on a plane
I don't like the weather when it's freezing
Because I catch a cold and start sneezing
I can't wait for the summer sun
Because it will be a lot more fun.

Natalie Pascual (12)
Pitreavie Primary School

Winter

To school I was told to go
Went out to find lots of snow
Soon a blizzard struck the air
And all I did was stand and stare
And think of all the wonderful things
That winter always seems to bring
Snowmen, sledging, snowball fights galore
The children just want more and more
The school bell rings, 'I'm late!'
The teacher waits to decide my fate
Just then the head comes through the door
'School's off!
There's no need to be here anymore.'

Ross Ritchie (11)
Pitreavie Primary School

The Winter Freeze

I'm lying under lots of sheets
Still trying to get a heat
Outside the street is icy
Tripping people up unnecessarily
Icicles hang off the trees
A lot of people start to sneeze
Sledging on the icy hill
Playing with our friends in the season of goodwill
The ducks can't get in the frozen pond
So they need a helping hand
But nobody's in a frosty mood
Because the winter weather is good.

Ryan Headrick (11)
Pitreavie Primary School

A Winter's Day

The snow outside is falling
Happy children are calling
Winter is here, cold winds blow
The lawn is no more green, but now covered in snow

Snowmen standing outside
Children having toboggan rides
All wrapped up in warm clothes
Warm and cosy like nobody knows

Hot drinks for everyone
Since there is no blazing sun
All in the house, warm and snug
Everyone with their cocoa mug.

Laura Duncan (11)
Pitreavie Primary School

My Mum

My mum is smart
my mum is funny
when she tries to tickle my tummy.

She always says she loves me
and I love her too
at night she gives me one big hug
and I give her one too.

A mum is someone who is always there
morning, noon and night
and with my mum
I have to say that
that is so, so right.

Leah Devaney (10)
St Bride's RC Primary School, Cowdenbeath

My Big Brother

In the morning, he's like a half-shut knife
Spends half an hour in the shower
And we always shout him out.
Tall and thin
Says nasty things
Thinks he's tough, even though he is not.
Fights with me
But never wins
Always gets in trouble
But says it's not his fault.
Eats like a pig
But says he does not.
He always gets detention
And hates doing homework.
He loves expensive things
Though never spends his money.
I love my brother
He can be nice.
He says I look good
And all those things.
I wouldn't swap him
Well, maybe I would. Hee hee!

Kira Grant (10)
St Bride's RC Primary School, Cowdenbeath

Guy Fawkes Night

As the twisters twirl up,
The shooting stars shoot,
The sparklers go crack,
Guy Fawkes night is back,

When I go past the bonfire,
I feel all its heat,
There's the bark of a hound,
The Catherine wheel goes round,

Up go the rockets,
With a boom and a bang!
There's bright colours in the sky,
Now my poem's ended,
It's time to say goodbye.

Alana Jones (10)
St Bride's RC Primary School, Cowdenbeath

Christmas Stocking

What will go into the Christmas stocking,
While the clock on the mantelpiece goes tick-tocking?
A packet of cars
And two Mars bars
A sugar mouse
And a little house
A football
I can kick off the wall
PS2 games
Please give me them all
A Game Boy advanced game
And a hard one, please
A Hotwheels track
And a puppet called Mac.
Come morning, you'll wake to the clock's tick-tocking,
And that's what you'll find in the Christmas stocking.

Martin McCormack (10)
St Bride's RC Primary School, Cowdenbeath

Bonfire Night

On a dark night, with bright stars shining down
Rainbow, shooting and all of that all in the sky
Children laughing and crying, I'm getting happier
Dogs jumping in the sky like a rocket
Whoosh went the traffic lights
Hmmm went my belly when I saw food
Rainbows in the sky
Pop, pop, pop went the fireworks
The smell of gunpowder made me sick
Dark smoke makes me dirty all over
So altogether it was a good day.

Michael Kemp (10)
St Bride's RC Primary School, Cowdenbeath

Christmas Stocking

What will go into the Christmas stocking
While the clock on the mantelpiece goes tick-tocking?

Chocolate bars
Sweeties in jars
Packet of pencils
A selection of stencils
Things for hair
And a necklace to wear
Candy sticks
That don't make me sick
Some colouring pens
Maybe ten
A bottle of party glitter
And a toy babysitter

Come morning, you'll wake to the clock's tick-tocking,
And that's what you'll find in the Christmas stocking.

Rachael Gibb (10)
St Bride's RC Primary School, Cowdenbeath

My Mum

My mum is tall and very thin,
she has a small nose and a normal chin.

She has blonde hair and blue eyes,
sometimes she gives me a big surprise.

My mum can cook very well,
I even get hypnotised by the wonderful smell.

My mum likes to go to the shop,
last time she bought a bucket and mop.

My mum likes to sit in the sun,
drinking her coffee and eating her bun.

My mum buys more than she really needs,
like sweets and toys and puppy-dog leads.

My mum puts a lot of bubbles in the bath,
and closes the window so there isn't a draught.

When my mum's wrong, she makes a funny comment,
so that she isn't a torment.

My mum drinks coffee all the time,
it's what makes her adult time sublime.

My mum loves me more than anything,
I bring her joy more than anyone can ever bring.

Samantha Drummond (10)
St Bride's RC Primary School, Cowdenbeath

Christmas Stocking

What will go into the Christmas stocking,
While the clock on the mantelpiece goes tick-tocking?

A little mini-telly,
And a wee pair of wellies,
A packet of cars,
That zoom away far,
A big coloured ball,
And a dolly called Molly,
A world full of love,
And a little toy dove,
Some pennies, not too many,
A book and a pair of socks,
And a small butcher's shop,
Red love hearts,
And some cream tarts,
We've had lots of fun,
But now it's all done.

Come morning, you'll wake to the clock's tick-tocking,
And that's what you'll find in the Christmas stocking.

Susan Miller (10)
St Bride's RC Primary School, Cowdenbeath

Chess Cinquain

Waiting
For it to move.
The bishop draws nearer.
It stops upon the dreaded square.
Check mate.

Finlay Dick (11)
St Columba's Primary School, Cupar

Man Utd Tanka

Football is great fun,
Man U - the best team ever.
Giggs plays on the left,
While Van Nistelrooy scores goals.
But Ronaldo is my fave!

Michael Hill (11)
St Columba's Primary School, Cupar

Space Tanka

Big, black and scary,
Jupiter is the biggest.
Planets everywhere,
Revolving round the big sun,
Never stopping to take rests.

James Russell (11)
St Columba's Primary School, Cupar

World War II Tanka

In the cold trenches
There is a war all around.
Nazis fight with Brits.
The people are rationing,
Hunger is seen everywhere.

Michael Linford (11)
St Columba's Primary School, Cupar

School Tanka

People don't like school
It is such a boring place
You just want to sleep!
In a cocoon, warm and safe
Nothing but sweet dreams all day.

Kristie Brown (11)
St Columba's Primary School, Cupar

Animals Cinquain

Snails hide,
Wolves are hiding,
Hyenas screeching loud,
Monkeys swinging on stringy vines,
Owls sleep.

Rachel Anderson (11)
St Columba's Primary School, Cupar

Winter Tanka

I am very cold.
Watching snowy icicles
Always makes me think
Of Christmas, laughter and joy.
I love winter, but do you?

Hope K Smith (11)
St Columba's Primary School, Cupar

Taz

My dog is called Taz,
He has big, brown and black paws.
He is very big.
I love him with all my heart,
He is my little angel!

Ben Logan (11)
St Columba's Primary School, Cupar

Mars

Raging like a dragon
Like a big bolt of fire
Boiling like an oven
Violent as a Roman soldier

Destructive as a shark
Burning like a devil
Courageous as Indiana Jones
Storming like a giant

Dangerous as a tiger
Pounding like a heartbeat
Fierce as an elephant
Shining like a bright star
Hot as a cooker.

Matthew Anderson (10)
St Columba's Primary School, Cupar

Red

Blood dripping from a dagger
A girl screams with fear
Like the bully planet called Jupiter
Its evil eyes rage
Red, the colour filled with anger.

Jonathon Morris (10)
St Columba's Primary School, Cupar

The Smallest Planet

Bigger than a mouse
Peacefully spinning
Quiet as a pencil mark on the table
Cold as a freezing vanilla ice cream
Nine planets away from the boiling sun
Pluto.

Naomi Maguire (9)
St Columba's Primary School, Cupar

My Planet Jupiter

J ourneys angrily around the sun, other planets run away
    from the big bully.
U p in space like a big ball of gas.
P owerfully blinding, pretty as a newborn puppy.
I inside you could fit all the other planets.
T wisting gradually like a graceful swan.
E xcited because he's big.
R aging storms in Jupiter's huge great eye and fire balls coming out.

Kayleigh Fusco Boyd (9)
St Columba's Primary School, Cupar

The Rocky Planet

M aybe a comet landing site
E arth is two doors away
R ocky unlike Saturn
C rashing comets hit its deserted surface
U nlike Pluto who is frozen
R unning around boasting about being closest to the sun
Y et Venus is the hottest planet.

Ciaran Russell (9)
St Columba's Primary School, Cupar

Where In The World?

How did Saturn get his rings?
Jupiter gave them to him as a present.

Are there Martians out there?
I don't know, have you seen one?
I'd like to see one, wouldn't you?

I wonder why the sun formed?
Maybe a devil escaped from Hell releasing his anger,
Or maybe not.

Why do the planets orbit the sun?
Could they want more of the Christmas cake?

Is there a tenth planet?
Who knows?

Where in the world?
This universe I'm in.

Calum Hawkins (9)
St Columba's Primary School, Cupar

A Very Lonely, Upset Planet

Pluto is
as cold as snow
as grey as a rabbit
as small as a golf ball
as hard to see as your nose
so gracefully Pluto slowly spins
248 years to orbit the sun
Pluto is a very lonely, upset planet
Pluto has no friends you see
Come on down Pluto and play
with me!

Jemma White (9)
St Columba's Primary School, Cupar

A Ball In Space

J ust like a ball of fiery catastrophic gas.
U p in space like a raging, mad giant.
P lace of destruction and exploding like a crater's landing.
I t's like a place of death and suffocation.
T earing its journey round the boiling, scorching sun.
E ye of fiery gas like a person's death.
R aging in space like the king of the universe.

Fhiona Dorrans (9)
St Columba's Primary School, Cupar

Green

A crocodile in the swamps
Near the River Nile
Stealthily swimming through the marsh
Searching for his prey in the fast, running water.

The summertime in the year,
With grass all round the town.

Celtic winning the SPL,
That would be a sight!

Patrick McAndrew (9)
St Columba's Primary School, Cupar

Grey

A dusty night as gas and smoke choke the innocent,
Ghosts mourning and floating about with guilt,
(They're about to go through their death day again.)
Bare trees die as their spirits restlessly howl in the wind,
Moshers smoke and drink in a plague-ridden town,
The cobwebs on a bloodstained dagger,
It's about to wake and kill its next victim.

Lauren Kennedy (9)
St Columba's Primary School, Cupar

Red

Blood gushing from an open, infected wound
Anger rushing to my head
A flaming house, the fire never-ending
Devil burning from the everlasting Hell
Roses scattered, no love around
Red sky in the morning, shepherd's warning
Outrage, poisoning a newborn baby
Brutal and beastly, stabbing hearts
Breathless and stuck underground
Excitement flattened by death and destruction
Veins in my body turning my face and hands black.

Nicky Wilson (9)
St Columba's Primary School, Cupar

Jupiter

J upiter is the king of the planets.
U nusual colours surround Jupiter.
P eacefully swirling around the sun as the king does.
I rritating all the other planets because he's boasting about himself.
T aking his journey around the sun still going on about how big he is.
E verything else except the sun is smaller than Jupiter.
R ed as blood is the great red spot.

Shona Larg (9)
St Columba's Primary School, Cupar

The Lonely Planet

Lonely planet miles from the sun
Needs to have a friend, he does
Chilly and freezing, so cold I can't breath
Orbiting the sun in 248 years
Mysterious, tiny Pluto away in the darkness.

Kim Cartwright (9)
St Columba's Primary School, Cupar

A Silent Poem

It was so quiet that I could hear
the eight legs of a spider
running across the ground.

It was so peaceful that I could hear
the trees breathing in and out
in and out.

It was so quiet that I could hear
the dust collecting up
on the bookshelves.

It was so peaceful that I could hear
the paint drying slowly
on the paper.

It was so quiet that I could hear
the plants transforming
into the most wonderful flowers.

It was so silent that I could hear
the gentle ripple in the water
at the pond.

It was so peaceful that I could hear
the plaster crumbling off the wall
in the classroom.

It was so silent that I could hear
the spider carefully knitting her web of glass beads
that shone in the sun's sparkling light.

Bronach Hughes (9)
St Columba's Primary School, Cupar

The Big Gliding Planet

Just the gigantic peaceful planet
Up in the huge universe,
Pirouetting gracefully round the boiling sun,
Into dark, glittering skies.
The great red spot creates incredible storms and hurricanes
Full of gases.
Exciting things happen on Jupiter.
Red skies like blood surrounding Jupiter.

Taylor Dow (9)
St Columba's Primary School, Cupar

Venus

V ery hot, the hottest planet
E arth people would get squashed
N o rivers or seas on Venus
U ntidy Venus is with its volcanoes
S ome people call Venus Earth's twin sister.

Paige Bain (9)
St Columba's Primary School, Cupar

Saturn

S aturn's gassy surface
A nd the sixth planet from the sun
T urning peacefully across the orbit
U nlike Earth the third planet from the sun
R ings of ice and rock, stone-cold as a block
N ot another planet like Saturn.

Megan Lonie (9)
St Columba's Primary School, Cupar

Apple

Apple
Green sphere
Round, hard, seeds
I can eat it all day
Excellent.

Ceri-Ann Newlands (7)
St Columba's Primary School, Cupar

Jupiter Is The Planet Of . . .

Jupiter is the planet of
white and orange clouds
full with magnificent
lightning.

Jupiter is the planet of
calm, slow and spins
all day long
peacefully.

Jupiter is the planet of
kings, ordering everyone about
balls of fire
gases.

Jupiter is the planet of
a lovely, beautiful surface
with a huge
spot.

Jupiter is the father of
Mars, and friends of
Saturn and Uranus and
Neptune.

Amy Winter (9)
St Columba's Primary School, Cupar

Down To Earth

The
Earth is round
The Earth is green and blue
Orbiting the sun calmly but swiftly;
The only planet with life. Twirling and
Twisting all way round the boiling, scorching sun
In 365 days. Her neighbour wonderful Venus
And Mars, she's fantastic, magnificent,
Wonderful and beautiful, the
Wateriest planet you
Could find. That's
Our Earth.

Aileen O'Hagan (9)
St Columba's Primary School, Cupar

A Big Red Balloon

King of the planets,
Massive, vast, gigantic, gas giant,
Bloodshot, evil eye watching over the solar system,
He thinks that he owns everything in the universe,
Courageously and destructively, raging like a dragon,
Jupiter bashes its way round the scorching, hot sun.
Striding about boasting and insulting everything he sees,
A rock hard centre (or a rock hard heart)
Scary, terrifying, revolting and rude.
What a big bully!

Margaret Mellon (9)
St Columba's Primary School, Cupar

The Red Spot

J upiter king of the planets.
U nbelievably massive,
P owerfully storming in the orbit of space.
I t's like a gigantic ball of fire.
T he evil red giant's eye glows in the dark like blood.
E legantly swirling in and out of the planets.
R aging like a dragon in space.

Lewis Souter Hogg (9)
St Columba's Primary School, Cupar

Red

Burning in my heart like fire
Evil blood travelling through my anger
Scared to move in the hole of terror
Trying to catch my breath.

Love swiftly surrounds the rose of friendship
Blushing with embarrassment
I was given a heart.

Jasmine Reilly (8)
St Columba's Primary School, Cupar

Banana

Banana,
Soft, big,
Juicy, sweet, yellow,
Nice and tastes good,
Banana.

Damian Day (7)
St Columba's Primary School, Cupar

Apple

Red, hard,
Good for teeth.
I like the taste.
Yum-yum.

Denis Potter (7)
St Columba's Primary School, Cupar

Apple

Apple
Red, hard
Circular seeds soft
Big, juicy
Yummy.

Adelle Melley (7)
St Columba's Primary School, Cupar

Can You Guess?

What is half moon shape,
Yellow with brown polka dots.
It has a secret zip and is soft inside.
Now it's open take a bite.
Have you guessed?
It's a *banana.*

Brogan McDonagh (7)
St Columba's Primary School, Cupar

Peach

Peach
Round, soft
Squiggy, yummy
Black stone inside
Good.

Kevin Small (8)
St Columba's Primary School, Cupar

Apple

Apple,
green, tasty,
nice and hard.
It is really juicy,
sweet.

Andrew Mellon (7)
St Columba's Primary School, Cupar

Orange

Orange
dotty, smooth
smells like wine
I could live on oranges
delicious.

Jemma Steele (7)
St Columba's Primary School, Cupar

Pomegranate

Pomegranate,
bound, rough,
hard, tough, heavy,
I just love them,
delicious.

Nicole Lambert (7)
St Columba's Primary School, Cupar

Apple

Apple,
Round, juicy,
Hanging from a tree,
Seeds inside,
Apple.

Christina Meiklem (7)
St Columba's Primary School, Cupar

Melon

It is rock hard.
It is yellow.
It is bumpy.
It is oval.
It is sweet.
It is yummy.

Emma Scott (7)
St Columba's Primary School, Cupar

Apple

Hard, smooth,
crunchy, red, juicy,
I could eat one twice a day.

Andrew Dorrans (7)
St Columba's Primary School, Cupar

Apple

Apple
Red and green, hard
Smooth, juicy, solid
It can roll, a sphere
I like the taste
Good, yummy.

Sarah Shanks (7)
St Columba's Primary School, Cupar

Melon

Heavy, hard,
Smooth, oval shaped,
Big, solid, rough bottom,
Smells like banana,
Delicious.

Daniel Levett
St Columba's Primary School, Cupar

Apple

Apple,
Round, smooth,
Soft, solid, hard.
It is very juicy.
Delicious.

Robert Douglas (7)
St Columba's Primary School, Cupar

Grapes

Grapes are juicy,
Soft and greeny,
Smooth,
Great to eat,
I like them in banana splits.

Cameron Durie (7)
St Columba's Primary School, Cupar

Orange

Orange,
hard,
rough,
round,
smooth.
I like the taste.

Anthony Pringle (7)
St Columba's Primary School, Cupar

Planes - Haiku

Planes take off quickly.
They straighten up in the sky.
One by one they land.

Robbie Laing (11)
St Columba's Primary School, Cupar

Orange

Orange,
hard, orange,
juicy, sphere, dotty,
tastes like wine,
lovely.

Jamie Laing (7)
St Columba's Primary School, Cupar

Pomegranate

Pomegranate,
Seedy sphere,
Juicy, hard, peachy,
I love to eat it,
Delicious.

Max Larg (7)
St Columba's Primary School, Cupar

Banana

Banana,
black, yellow,
soft, curly, fruity,
smells like wine, tasty,
delicious.

Patrick Williams (7)
St Columba's Primary School, Cupar

Melon

Melon,
Big, rough,
Loads of seeds,
It tasted juicy and smooth,
Best fruit in the world,
Melon.

Harry Winter (7)
St Columba's Primary School, Cupar

World War II

Nineteen thirty-nine
World War II has started now
Hitler was in charge
He bombed Britain more than once
But Britain won World War II.

Iain Wilson (11)
St Columba's Primary School, Cupar

Space

Comets flashing through the sky
Spilt hot gold mustard paint
Never-ending
Fierce sun
A light bulb flashing, rotating
Light encasing
Planets around the sun.

Jasmine Wilson (9)
St Leonards Middle School, St Andrews

Saturn

Orange, dark and light
Mix in the night
Rings of eight
I have no mate
But brothers and sisters eight
Mercury 1, Venus 2, Earth 3
Mars 4, Jupiter 5, Uranus 7,
Neptune 8, and last and smallest
Pluto
But one is missing
I am Saturn
Who fills the gap.

Mary Ann McKechnie (10)
St Leonards Middle School, St Andrews

My Moon Dream

Sun, ball of boiling hot water
Stars like sparks of diamonds
Every night I dream of space
I am flying through the shooting stars
It's dark like a power cut
I track my way to the moon
Bouncing, pouncing
My moon dream.

Hannah Gray (8)
St Leonards Middle School, St Andrews

The Planet I Love The Most

The planet I love the most
Is like a ball of cheese
I wish I could visit!

Bright orange with a ragged surface
With a ring of silver circling it
I wish I could visit!

Have you thought of which planet it is?
Yes, it is Saturn. The ring round Saturn
Is a light silver and very thin!

It looks lovely
I wish I could visit it!

Joanna MacKay (10)
St Leonards Middle School, St Andrews

The Big Bang

100 million years ago
Where nothing was,
Something happened.
There was a bang,
Not just any bang,
An absolutely mind-blowing blast of a *bang!*
Of dark energy.
Where there was nothing,
There is now an elemental
Energy of eternal power.

Robert Clark (9)
St Leonards Middle School, St Andrews

Beagle 50

When Beagle 50 finally fell on the Red Planet,
It was like a millennium.
Everyone in Britain was celebrating.
They had made it to the Red Planet.

The Americans thought
It was a bit too late.
But that didn't dampen
The British spirit.
Because they had made it to
The Red Planet.

But one thing they didn't know:
That Beagle 50 fell apart on the Red Planet.

Josh Jamieson (10)
St Leonards Middle School, St Andrews

The Big Bang

In the black, dark, deserted desert
That we call space
All was very silent
Until a loud
Bang!

Planets were forming
I stand here and wonder
Is space any different
To a vandalised park
With cans?
Space with little and big
Pieces of metal floating.

A comet zooms by
Like a cricket ball
I stand here and wonder
Is space any different
From an empty street?
A few lights glittering
Space with lots of stars.

Cameron Spencer (9)
St Leonards Middle School, St Andrews

Black Ebony Sky

Necklace of stars across the
Black ebony sky
That's my world of space

Comets leaving Milky Ways across the
Black ebony sky
That's my space world

Mars streaks like a rose across the
Black ebony sky
My world of space.

Charlotte Lorimer (8)
St Leonards Middle School, St Andrews

Space

Stars stand in the darkness,
Moon shining upon them,
Following us as we go along,
Walking backwards,
In the dark.

Danny Stewart (8)
St Leonards Middle School, St Andrews

Out There

Out there in the never-ending darkness
A billion stars glitter like the moon on the sea.

Out there uncountable planets lie untouched
Waiting to be found.

Out there are deadly aliens
Planning to take over planets.

Out there comets fly around
Disintegrating as they hit the Earth's atmosphere.

Out there are huge space stations
Discovering more about space.

Out there floats space debris;
Rusting rockets or past probes.

Out there shooting stars
Entertain us with their speed and light.

Out there is the sun
Its boiling gases are a dragon's breath.

Out there a black hole lies
Waiting with its hungry mouth.

Out there in the never-ending darkness . . .

Zak Maas (10)
St Leonards Middle School, St Andrews

Bodie

B odie, called after Boudicia.
O utstanding cat.
D iscovered my love for cats.
I ntelligent mouser.
E ntered my life when I entered life.

Olivia Gibson (8)
St Leonards Middle School, St Andrews

Dark Energy

Dark energy - a plough,
Through space.

A ball of unknown power,
A magnetic shield hovering,
Earth's garbage getting pushed out of the way,
A broom sweeping dust,
A flat, white ball,
Like wax from a flame.

A gateway to the afterlife
For all lost souls,
Their black tunnel.

Drifting round the stars,
A spark in the dark, somehow alive.
Forever watching planets.
A mind of its own,
A mirror of darkness
And a spy for space.

Richard Ward (9)
St Leonards Middle School, St Andrews

Speedy Planets

Silently space moves its way round the sun.
Suddenly, Saturn's rings decide to go speedier.
All of a sudden, it's going quicker than the blink of an eye.

It clashes into Mars, Jupiter, then Neptune.
Soon they are zooming.
The scientists' good work is one for.
There is nothing to do except send someone up there.

He is sent up in a magnificent spaceship
With a massive robot-snatching hand that catches
Any planet.

He grabs Saturn and slows it down.
Now they are going 24 hours instead of four.

He flies back to Earth with his mission accomplished
And truly enough they are all full of glee.
Oh space ranger! Won't you teach me?

Natalie De Groot (9)
St Leonards Middle School, St Andrews

Sweet Solar System

Golden, twinkling Smarties
The Milky Way full of chocolate
Galaxy black as liquorice
Stars are bright as fireflies
What a yum, yum space.

Nina Duncan (8)
St Leonards Middle School, St Andrews

Space Box

In my dad's tool box
Is another world.

The sandpaper is
The rough foundations on Mars.
The screwdrivers are spaceships
Trying to seek out other worlds.
The measuring tapes are
The sticky, smooth tongues
Of bloodsucking aliens.
The drill sounds like shooting stars,
Shooting, whizzing, flooding past you.

When you open the rusty lid
You walk into another world.

Space.

The nails are old, lost satellites
Looking for their base.
The wire is the rings around Saturn
Full of gasses.

Every time my dad opens his toolbox
I play astronauts
And pretend that
I am in my favourite place,
Space!

Alice Ferguson (10)
St Leonards Middle School, St Andrews

Moon, Pluto, Mars

Moon
Are you lonely moon, by yourself up there?
You have no plants or trees or flowers
Your soil is only rocks and glass
But please don't cry
For I still love you in the sky

Pluto
What do you do Pluto, all alone up there?
You are as blue as a blueberry
And you have no water or air
No wonder nothing lives up there
But don't go now
For I still love you in the sky

Mars
Are you lonely Mars, all alone up there?
You have already vanquished all your enemies
I thought you were frightened
But you fight like a rhino
I wish you were normal
And had many friends
But please don't march away
For I still love you in the sky.

Alexander Murray (10)
St Leonards Middle School, St Andrews

Deep In Space

Deep, deep in we see . . .

The sun sparkles like gold
And the silver stars twinkle.
The planets are like footballs.
Space is full of black energy
And everlasting darkness.
Saturn is like a pebble in water.

Deep, deep in space.

Ged Rutherford (9)
St Leonards Middle School, St Andrews

Young Writers - Once Upon A Rhyme Fife

In The Wilderness

In the wilderness,
the moon is a velvety guard,
like a glinting new golf ball.
It reflects the sun's dancing rays.
The moon's friendly face
watches as the ruby-red planet
plays in the twinkling sparks.

In the wilderness
Pluto lies lonely,
far out from the warm sun.
It sits as a secret never to be uncovered.
It swims in the floating stars,
like a frozen raindrop.

In the wilderness
Jupiter proudly sits
as king of the planets.
Delicately painted in
golden gasses
his superior face
is hidden by secrecy.

In the wilderness
the sun's velvety surface
is an infinite night light
for the Milky Way,
as it warms the planets' faces for eternity.
Our rumbling ball of fire
just drifts in the wilderness.

Flora Ogilvy (9)
St Leonards Middle School, St Andrews

Space

In a lost, deserted space
Far, far away
Lie only stars,
Which look like dot after dot.
If you are unlucky
You will be sucked into a sudden death
By a bottomless black hole
And disappear for good.

In a lost, deserted space
Far, far away
Lie only stars
Which look like dot after dot.
If you are lucky
You will drift and drift
For a year,
But then you see a string
Of planets,
Our solar system.

Izak Maas (9)
St Leonards Middle School, St Andrews

Space Probes

When space probes are launched,
the world is excited
trying to see if there is life on Mars.

Space probes land, like an aeroplane drifting down.
Giant inflatable bubbles appear.
A machine powered by many people on Earth
trying to see if there is life on Mars.

Back on Earth,
everyone waits for a signal to be made.
Hoping to see pictures of the Red Planet,
trying to see if there is life on Mars.

Sara Aguilar (10)
St Leonards Middle School, St Andrews

What's Beyond?

What's beyond that bright blue sky?
Those fluffy clouds travelling by?

Many majestic objects that sky conceals
Like a dazzling night star, the queen of the show,
With her pure light dancing, she bewilders all.

The moon, she shines reflecting light,
Her dusty surface possesses a true might.

A deep black hole, the gangster of the night,
No mercy he holds, destroying all grand light.

The warrior Mars, true king of them all,
His power everlasting, ruling with might.
His cruelty reigns, every stretch of space known,
All who see him fear, their faces turn white.

What's beyond that bright blue sky,
Have you ever wondered why?

Liam Deboys (11)
St Leonards Middle School, St Andrews

Soft Space

Soft, feather stars
Space mountain
Floating gently
Blue planet twinkling
Flaking, floating, moon walking
Astronaut
It is fun to see you fly
In the sky.

Holly Milne (8)
St Leonards Middle School, St Andrews

Floating In Space

Galaxies in the night sky
Twiddling stars
Quiet in the dark
Meteors zooming across the blackness
Astronauts hovering in the space
Black holes sucking in stars
Closing up
Glowing hot sun shining down
Planet Earth, the most beautiful of all.

Jamie Morse (8)
St Leonards Middle School, St Andrews

The Black Hole

The black hole
Is not like the sun
Nor like bitter Pluto
It is a passageway.

The passage is made
Of air, not any air
Not air we breathe
The air made of the strongest
Iron and rock.

But what is beyond?

A passageway made
Of the strongest iron
And rock.

Is it Heaven with its angels for messengers?
Or is it the place filled
With fire and rage
That is called Hell?

But what is beyond?
Beyond is unknown.

Victoria Baillie (10)
St Leonards Middle School, St Andrews

My Little Ones

I have nine little ones
Mercury, Venus
Saturn and Uranus
Are each twins
Earth, Mars, Jupiter, Neptune
And Pluto has beautiful skins.

The moons calls me Sun
And so do the stars
Milky Way and Galaxies
But my little planets call me Sunny.

I am the biggest of the universe
Everyone respects me as they spin
Forward around my body
Never in reverse.

Saturn has seven rings around him
1, 2, 3, 4, 5, 6 and 7
No wonder he is always late
He bought a few too many rings
Which he got in Tescos
On planet Zoo Ding.

Stars are the navy
Always fighting at night-time
But planets think space is a swimming pool
My little ones are my favourite set
They are definitely my personal pets
Come look
Mercury is my newest baby born.

Charlotte Lindesay-Bethune (10)
St Leonards Middle School, St Andrews

Everlasting Darkness

In the everlasting darkness,
Nine planets glow bright,
A weightless astronaut travels by,
To witness the wonderful sight.

Through the stars and through the comets,
The planet Pluto lies,
It's freezing frosty surface,
Drowns away its squealing cries.

Arranged in perfect order,
The nine planets are
Like a line of boys at Scout camp,
Travelling out afar.

Mars, red and flaming,
Venus, warm and dry,
'We're too strange for any human life,'
All the planets sigh.

In the everlasting darkness,
Everything is silent,
No noise, no sound, no hearing,
As nothing is violent.

Iain Watson (10)
St Leonards Middle School, St Andrews

The Milky Way

I always thought someone
Took 100 cows to space,
But when my eye looked up in the sky,
I banged into a lamp post,
And right then and there
Things started making sense,
The Milky Way is someone
Pouring milk into a hole.

The white milk goes faster
And faster, as it pours down,
The deep, dark drain.
But at the end of this drain,
Spiders live and play.
I would not like to be
That carton of milk!

Louise Cox (10)
St Leonards Middle School, St Andrews

Day Trip To Space

What's beyond space out there?
Meteors, asteroids everywhere.
The moon, the stars, who knows?
Where's Mars?
What do you see on a day trip to space?

What do you see on a day trip to space?
Pass the planets, through the sky,
Look, there's spacemen plodding by.
What do you see on a day trip to space?
Venus, Saturn, Uranus and Neptune,
As I pass, I whistle a tune.
Oh quick, quick, I cannot stop,
What do you see on a day trip to space?

That's what I see.

Annabel Zajicek (9)
St Leonards Middle School, St Andrews

Look, Look Carefully From A Rocket

Look, look carefully from a rocket,
Look, see all the wonderful worlds in space.
See the delicious Milky Way floating
And escaping Earth's ravenous mouth.

Look, look carefully from a rocket,
Look, find the fireflies which fly clumsily,
Bashing into objects.
Look for the planets and try to find the aliens
With triangular eyes.

Can you see them try to take a meteor ride?
Beware, for if you look carefully,
You will see a big, boisterous, black hole
Which sucks in anything in reach!

Look, look carefully from a rocket,
If you look very hard, you might just see
The Snitch from Harry Potter,
But it is the great, golden gates
Which lead to Heaven.
Take a closer look,
You will see fine, gold embroidered decorated swans.

Look, look carefully from a rocket,
Look, see all the wonderful words in space.

Amber Wilson (10)
St Leonards Middle School, St Andrews

The Eye Of Pluto

The eye of Pluto sees
A procession of planets
Leading to the sun,
But he can't understand
Why Mercury won't let him lead
Just for once

The eye of Pluto
Can't see far,
Because he is at the
End of the long traffic jam.

The eye of Pluto
Tries to see what's happening
Far ahead of him,
He tries looking left, also right,
Up and down but he catches
Not even a glimpse of Uranus.
No wonder he can't see Mercury or Venus,
The eye of Pluto can't see the sun.

Emily Allen (10)
St Leonards Middle School, St Andrews

Contrasting Cats

Glamorous white cat
It walks like a model
Fashion strides
Living on skimmed milk
And best tuna fish.

Sad, dirty, grey cat
It walks like a tramp
Living on water
And leftovers.

Lily Ratcliff (8)
St Leonards Middle School, St Andrews

The Potion

I'm in a little shop
With lots of little jars
They're full of different liquids
That I think are medicines.

I've got a cold you see
I take one off the shelf
I take out the cork
And pop it in my mouth.

'Ah! That feels better,' I say to myself
Oh! Now what's happening?
Upwards I am floating
Crash . . . through the roof I go.

I'm soaring over treetops like a little bird
Oh no! Where am I going?
The Earth is falling downwards
Or am I going up?

Next second, I'm passing Mars
Oh and there's Jupiter
It's getting rather dark.

Wow! What was that bright light?
I think it was a shooting star
Now here comes Saturn with its rings around it
Here comes Uranus and Neptune
It's very cold up here, I think I've got frostbite.

There's Pluto, last but not least
Wow! There are little people on Pluto
I want to go and meet them.

Flash . . . wow! I'm back in the shop
That was a super strong potion
And it made a good adventure
Achoo . . . but I still have my cold.

Cassia Littler (10)
St Leonards Middle School, St Andrews

Stars

White stars shooting fast
Over the blazing sun
Down to Earth as fast as it can
Through the dark night
Then
Boom!
Pieces of stars
Flying everywhere
People carefully catching
The glowing splinters of stars
Putting them softly
In a jar
Catching space in stars.

Keir Hunter (8)
St Leonards Middle School, St Andrews

The Race For Space

Down in the darkness of space
You can be in the place
Of the galaxy
The race of comets flying through the air
You need to keep up the pace to stay in space
The planet Earth in a race round the sun in space
The blue planet is managing to stay in the race
Saturn keeping up the pace to fly through the planets in space
Ships flying through the empty, black space
In the race for space.

Fraser Gillan (8)
St Leonards Middle School, St Andrews

Jumping Through Galaxies

Walking on stars
Seeing galaxies
Jumping on Jupiter
Escaping from Saturn
Finding Mars
Hearing echoes in space
Smelling silver neon dust
Tasting candyfloss air
Touching stars in space.

Angus Littleford (8)
St Leonards Middle School, St Andrews

Space

Astronauts swooping from the black everlasting space
Suits of white matching the stars
Landing on Mars
Getting colder and colder
Like Christmas tree lights hanging still
Not a sound can be heard

Large, fiery ball too hot to touch or go near
Brightest in the galaxy
Too hot to touch
Planets rotating round it
A beautiful sight to see
Mercury is the closest
But not hottest
Space goes on forever
It's as black as the night
Colours like rainbow
Christmas tree lights.

Katie Overend (8)
St Leonards Middle School, St Andrews

The Ghost

There was a ghost that liked to creep
And he did it in his sleep.
The ghost went into the hall
But was very small.

Because it was late it was dark,
The ghost bumped into Mark,
The boy screamed out loud and spun round and round,
The ghost was frightened of the sound.

They both ran back to their rooms,
And closed their doors with a boom,
They hid under their covers to wait for their brothers.

Liam Tarvit (10)
St Monans Primary School, St Monans

The Bloodsucking Vampire

The vampire is ready to suck the blood of an innocent girl,
He loves to drink the blood of a child,
He drinks all night till he's satisfied,
Then he goes out and goes very wild.

He is very thirsty,
He feels so weak,
He cannot wait till the night comes
And his hunger's at its peak.

The night is cold and dark,
The night is evil and creepy,
Keep your windows closed,
Whenever you are sleepy.

Megan Gilbert (10)
St Monans Primary School, St Monans

The Winter Is Here

The winter is here yet again,
We're all out playing on our skates and sliding on the ice,
Watch out, it's slippy, don't fall on your bum,
Because I did once or twice.

The snow has finished and we're all inside,
Cosy and warm with our pjs on,
We're going to our beds 'cause that's what Mum said,
To rest our tired, sleepy heads.

Lindzi Tarvit (10)
St Monans Primary School, St Monans

The Elephant

The elephant is a very big animal,
It's very big and tall,
One day it had a baby elephant
And it was very small.

Every day it grew bigger,
Right from head to toe,
The baby elephant was so cute,
Its mum had called it Moe.

Moe is big, she is ten years old,
She's played and had so much fun,
She's played right through the years,
But now it's time to leave her mum.

Rachael Clarke (10)
St Monans Primary School, St Monans

The Snow Blizzard

There once was a snow blizzard,
That nearly froze us all,
We all went out of school so we could play football,
Just then we heard the grit men.

They gritted everywhere but a bit more snow fell,
It was so exciting,
I ran home to play,
I went to my bed and the snow just faded away.

Douglas Hughes (9)
St Monans Primary School, St Monans

Spring

Spring is the season of both sun and rain
Spring is so calm and peaceful
Spring is the daffodil's birthday
Spring is when the house is cleaner.

Spring is the happy season
Spring is the best season ever for flowers
Spring is when the trees touch the top of towers
Spring is great because everything's so fresh.

Tyler King (10)
St Monans Primary School, St Monans

Tiger

One morning a tiger woke up and stretched,
He decided to go hunting,
He saw some zebras, stripy and fast,
Some of them were jumping.

He crouched low in the long, long grass,
Waiting to sneak up on his food,
He chased the zebra across the land,
He ate and was in a good mood.

Jordan McMullan (10)
St Monans Primary School, St Monans

The Big Snake

Once there was a snake,
Who lived at the edge of a lake,
He was slimy, stripy and spotty,
He had fangs like a sharp saw
And a head all dotty.

He wandered about the forest,
Looking for something to eat,
But slipped over someone's feet,
And went back down the toilet seat.

Graeme Guthrie
St Monans Primary School, St Monans

Seasons Of The Year

Spring is a season
When flowers grow,
Winter has gone
And so has the snow.

Summer is a season
When it starts to get hot,
I went to the beach,
How many people got there? A lot.

Autumn is a season
When the trees lose their leaves,
It starts to get cold
And the birds cross the seas.

Winter is a season,
Snow starts to fall,
Wrap up warm
Because this is winter's call.

Kiyrie McLellan (9)
St Monans Primary School, St Monans

The Snow

The snow so white and clean,
The snow, look at the gleam,
The snow is passing fast,
The snow, oh, it's stopping and starting.

The snow, look at it go,
The snow, it should be on show,
The snow, it's passing fast,
The snow, oh, it's stopping and starting.

The snow, it's turned to ice,
The snow, it's so nice,
The snow, it's passing fast,
The snow, it's melting at last.

(Until next winter!)

Ryan Leitch (9)
St Monans Primary School, St Monans

The Bully And The Bin

I'll tell you a story about a bully and a bin,
First I think I'll tell you what lies within,
A banana skin, an apple (complete with maggot) and a colony of ants,
A shoe, a tin can and an old pair of pants.

So once I was walking along minding my own,
When guess who turned up but my old enemy, evil Machound,
I tried to walk round but his goons showed up and grabbed me,
They threw me down to the ground.

So evil Machound picked me up and dragged me
To the edge of the playground,
No, I thought, *not the dreaded bin.*
But yes, head first down the bin.
So now I'm another thing that lies within.

Jamie Allen (10)
St Monans Primary School, St Monans

Thunder Kennings

Lightning flashes
Car bashes.

Thunder crashes
Rain splashes.

Thrashing branches
Wind dances.

Street light flashes
Person dashes.

Get home before the storm.

Stefan Fraser (11)
St Ninian's Primary School, Cardenden

Gold

Gold is like a sweet
tempting me to eat out of Quality Street.

Gold is the colour of a crown
worn by the wicked king around.

Gold is the colour of the sun
big and round and colourful and fun.

Gold is the colour of my hair
cool and smart and so is my friend.

Gold is the colour of the sand
flowing through and tickling my toes.

Gold is the colour of a medal
that you can win at your favourite sport.

Michael Donaldson (11)
St Ninian's Primary School, Cardenden

The Writer Of This Poem

(Based on 'The Writer Of This Poem' by Roger McGough)

The writer of this poem
is as good as gold.

He is like a cold cucumber.

He is as strong as a rock.

He is as clever as a fox.

He is like a sharp nail.

He is like a strong wind on a cold day.

He is as special as the Queen, or that is what they say.

He is as handsome as Orlando Bloom!

Christopher Inglis (11)
St Ninian's Primary School, Cardenden

Yellow

Yellow is like the sun,
Bright and warm.

Yellow is a melon,
Juicy and ripe.

Yellow is my mum's hair,
Beautiful and soft.

Yellow is my pen,
Bright and colourful.

Yellow is my jumper,
All nice and warm.

Sarah-Louise Mckie (11)
St Ninian's Primary School, Cardenden

Blue

Blue is like the feeling when you feel sad,
Blue is like a totally cool band that lives in our land,
Blue is like the bed sheets that lie upon my bed,
Blue are like the posters that sit above my head.
Blue is like the colour of the sky.

John Kay (11)
St Ninian's Primary School, Cardenden

School

S chool is a chore,
C razy and
H ot,
O ur lessons are many,
O ur life is hard,
L eaving school will be fab.

Nicole Curran (11)
St Ninian's Primary School, Cardenden

My Mum

Mum loves me,
Mum makes my tea.
After school she waits for me,
Then my sister pushes me.
Mum gets mad,
Then she tells Dad.

Owen Stewart (10)
Tayport Primary School

The M62

The school trip was a special occasion,
But we did not reach our destination,
Instead of the zoo,
I got stuck in the loo!
At the M62 service station.

The toilet started to leak,
I gave a big shriek!
Soon the water was up to my face,
I was in disgrace,
Then the door broke off,
I let out a cough,
Then we went back to school.

Danny Arnold (10)
Tayport Primary School

Dogs

Dogs can smell,
So can you.

Dogs can be cute,
So can you,
But only when you want to.

Dogs can bully,
So can you.

Dogs can be loud,
You can be too.

They cost a ton,
But you can have a lot of fun.

Kayleigh Paterson (11)
Tayport Primary School

Animals And You

Horses have hooves,
Dragons have wings,
I can think of many things.

Rabbits have ears,
So do you,
Can you think of more things too?

Hamsters are fuzzy
So is your hair,
People sometimes like to stare.

Cats have sharp claws
So they can scratch your drawers.
Thank goodness dogs have softer paws.

Sophie Brown (11)
Tayport Primary School

A Secret!

Down a secret path,
Through a secret wood,
To the shore of the secret sea.
I creep on tiptoe,
To the place I know,
That no one has seen except me,
Except me.
That no one has seen except me.

And the soft wind that blows
Through the roses
That I pass along the way,
Seems to whisper low,
But no one must know.
The secret you have learned today.

Jennifer Brown (11)
Tayport Primary School

My Mum

My mum makes my tea
My mum buys me sweets
My mum gets me toys
My mum is loving
My mum is caring
She loves me
And I love her.

Ross Noble (11)
Tayport Primary School

The Cat And The Rat

The cat is as fast
           as the rat
  the rat is as fast
           as the cat.
The cat is as fat
           as the rat
  the rat is as fat
           as the cat.

The cat has pointy ears
  the rat's are wee and round.
And when both are in the house,
  neither
    makes
      a
        sound!

Craig Bell (11)
Tayport Primary School

Playground On A Misty Day

Out playing at interval,
The mist was ungrateful,
Wetting us, freezing us, blinding us, deafening us,
Making us yearn for the bell.

Steven Lough (12)
Tayport Primary School

The Highlands And Lowlands

The Highlands are high,
The Lowlands
are
low.

The Highlands have heather,
The
Lowlands
have
weather.

In the Highlands, Wallace fought together with the heather.

The redcoats
lay
low
in the
Lowlands.
The Highlands had the flower of Scotland.

The heather called them all together, the fine Highland men.

Ben Parihar (10)
Tayport Primary School

My Little Sister

My little sister's really cute,
And she eats a lot of fruit.
Splish, splosh in her gravy,
Gulp, gulp, drinking like a baby.
Yell, yell, yes time for bed,
Nighty night, the time of dread!
'Argh,' she is crying for her teddy,
But now it's morning already.
She's awake, I hear her roaring,
I wish I was still just snoring.
Get her juice, hurry, hurry!
Enter our mum who calls her Honey.
Eat your breakfast up dear Charlotte,
But not so fast to make you scarlet!
My little sister's really great,
She really is my best mate!

Amy Jones (11)
Tayport Primary School

Drawer Of Doom

Every night when my drawer is in sight,
My face goes extremely white.
I have to get my clothes for tomorrow,
And I'm sure in there is a monster called Zorro.
I saw him once before when I peeked my head,
Into the drawer before I went to bed.
His body was bare,
But he had a head full of hair.
Now is the time to get out my clothes,
My body is shivering from my head to my toes.
I'm at my drawer . . . and he's got me!

Jade McRitchie (10)
Tayport Primary School

My Friend

I have a friend called Keri,
She has a teddy called Benny,
And Benny has a friend called Rocky.
Rocky is a bird and Keri is a girl.
But I have a friend called Keri, she is the best friend ever!

Louisa Reid (10)
Tayport Primary School

Tears

Tears
Tears are when I'm scared
They feel like knives cutting my
Skin.
They nip and taste like saltwater
They make my teeth stick like
Glue.
People, they ask me, 'What is
Wrong with you?'
I want to answer but the words
Just stay in my head.

The crowd gets bigger and
Bigger.
They swarm like bees
Surrounding me.
I hear the gossip, I hear the
Giggles.
I want to shout, 'Stop it now!'
But
No words come out.
Instead of words I have one thing

My tears!

Alice Minick (11)
Tayport Primary School

The Storm

The winds roar
The storms blow
The thunder crackles
All terror breaks loose.

People scream
People cry
People run for their lives
People stare
People hide
People wish the storm was over.

Some people love it!

Erica Lowe (10)
Tayport Primary School

Stars

I look into the sky at night,
And see the stars shine so bright.

There are many different names of stars,
There are also planets just like Mars.

Sirius the Dog Star is so bright,
It looks just like a light.

I looked to the sky to see one fall,
While I was sat on a high wall.

Stars are the souls of women and men,
Now I look to the stars again.

Dale Brownless (11)
Tayport Primary School

Square Eyes

One day my mum said to me,
'You'll get square eyes watching all that TV!'
But I didn't listen and kept on watching
And guess what happened to me.

The very next day I lay in my bed
With a sore head.
I looked in the mirror and gave a scream,
My face went as white as ice cream.

My mum heard me and came up,
She took one look and dropped her cup.
I watched too much TV
And this is what had happened to me.

I had square eyes!

Mum took me to the doctors
To see what they could do
But Dr Foster had gone to Gloucester
And no one knew what to do.

I went to bed that night
Looking very white.
My head was very sore
But I soon began to snore.

When I woke up in the morning
I looked in the mirror,
My eyes were round
So I made a sound.

It sounded like hip, hip, hooray!

Nell Glen   (11)
Tayport Primary School

When I Grow Up . . .

When I grow up . . . I'll be tall and thin,
Not too thin to be a pin!
I'll be swanky,
I'll be cool,
I'll even have my own swimming pool,
My job will be a hairdresser,
A make-up artist too,
And my bathroom, very posh, will have a very fancy loo!

When I grow up . . . I will love to sing,
And love to act on stage,
I'll marry a prince,
He'll become a king,
We'll never rant or rage,
We'll stay together for ever and ever,
And never hate each other.

Johanna Beat (11)
Tayport Primary School

My Cat

I have a cat called Spangle
She climbed up the tree next door
She really got in a tangle
Now she can't get down anymore!

She's really up so high,
She's making such a cry,
She's really in a mangle,
I think I'm going to strangle Spangle.

I hope she's going to get down,
I'm going to be worried all night
But when she gets down in the morning,
She's going to get a second warning!

Koren Anderson (11)
Tayport Primary School

Volcanoes

Puffs of smoke, chunks of rock
Don't go up there or you will burn your socks.
It is a black and red wine gum on an anthill melting in the sunlight.
I have to get out of here before it is too late,
Get over the bridge before it is too late,
Safe at last, nothing to worry about so let's
Have
A rest.

Michael Greig (11)
Tayport Primary School

2004

2004 will be a great year
I hope there will be no crying or fear
In 2004 there will be lots of sun
2004 will be such fun.

2004 will give us information on Mars
2004 will bring new fast cars
2004 will bring smiley faces
In 2004 we'll go to new places.

2004 is a new beginning
In 2004 there will be loads of singing
2004 has never been here before
So everyone don't let 2004 be a bore.

Catherine Carson (11)
Tayport Primary School

Friends

My friends are always there for me,
Whenever I am feeling down.
Take Arwen for instance,
She always backs me up,
Even when my life is blue,
She sticks to me like PVA glue.
If I'm ever feeling down,
Hayley turns my frown upside down.
And then there's my new friend,
Her name is Johanna,
If she put on yellow lipstick,
Her smile would look like a banana!

Charlotte Hanlon (11)
Tayport Primary School

Snail Adventure

On his way to the park
He slowly slithers along
All his friends run away
They say he has a pong.

He doesn't care that he has no friends
He keeps going on his way
He wants to get to the park
Even if it takes all day.

He goes in his shell if it gets too scary
He just has to be brave
He is so small
His shell is like a cave.

Three weeks later he arrives at the park
His friends he has to seek
He sees them on the swings
To get there may take a week.

Hayley Leitch (11)
Tayport Primary School

Valentine's Day

Roses are red
Violets are blue
Sugar is sweet
And so are you.

You sent me a rose
And I gave a pose
I don't even know who you are.

I must see you every day
Which makes me want to know
I sit and stare at who would look
But no one ever knows.

You are a great admirer
Really you are
I just want to know who you really are

Are you cool
Or are you smart?
Do you play football
In the park?

Roses are red
Violets are blue
You are so sweet
But I don't know you.

Gemma Gorham (11)
Tayport Primary School

Dundee FC Players

Jim Duffy,
He's the boss
Of the team.
If the players do
Something wrong,
He knows how to scream.

Barry Smith,
He's the captain of the squad,
I think he has done a very good job.
As we know our side is the better side,
Better than United's side.

Nacho Novo,
He is the best,
He knows it all.
You should see him do it all.
He really knows where to put the ball.
As I said, he's the best over all.

Lee Wilkie,
He is bald
But very tall.
He really knows how
To header that ball
As he is the tallest of them all.

Julian Speroni,
He is the goalie,
As he saves all the shots.
He doesn't mean to miss
A single shot,
But he is the best over all.

Morbheinn McTavish (11)
Tayport Primary School

What Is It?

Creeping silently under a chair
Eyeing its prey
What is it?
Blue eyes sparkle
And look at the hole
What is it?
A pink nose twitches
Suddenly it pounces
What is it?
It's a cat!

Fiona Macleod (10)
Tayport Primary School

I Like Snow

I like snow I think it's great,
I like to play in it with my mates,
I like it how it's nice and white,
And the way the sun shines on it makes it bright,
It's fun when you have a snowball fight,
When you hit someone they get a bit of a fright.

I like to build funny snowmen,
Since it's fun I do it again and again,
Building families big and small,
If they're too big they always fall.

When I'm sledging I enter the races,
When people fall off they land flat on their faces,
The thicker the snow, the faster you go,
I like doing the big step jumps,
But not going over the lumpy bumps.

Winter is the best time of the year,
Just because the snow is here.

Luke Driscoll (11)
Tayport Primary School

Heaper Peaper

Heaper Peaper chimney sweeper
Had a wife but could not keep her
Had another but did not love her
Up the chimney he did shove her.

Kevin Garlour (11)
Tayport Primary School

My Best Friend Julie

Julie and I are stuck like glue
You couldn't find better friends than us two.

She has lovely golden, wavy hair,
Bright blue eyes and a cheeky smile.

We have the best girls' days out
Swimming, shopping there's no doubt
Some people call us sisters when we are out
I'm not surprised, the way we act, it's like sisters
But we never fall out.

And when it comes to birthdays,
We always know what to get each other,
And she always buys the best presents ever,
We are the best, best friends ever.

We like the same music and the same style of clothes
And we both like to pose in front of a mirror.
One day we would like to get a flat together,
Just her and me.

If I had to describe her then I would say,
She is extremely funny, makes you laugh when you are upset,
And finally, not forgetting she is always ready to sort out a problem!

Hannah Sullivan (11)
Tayport Primary School

My Best Friend

My best friend is really sweet,
Even though he has no feet,
He has no arms, he has no head,
He doesn't sleep in a bed.

He's sometimes white, he's sometimes brown,
He doesn't smile, he doesn't frown,
He's sometimes square, he's sometimes round,
He never ever makes a sound.

He has his name on his clothes,
In a shop he likes to pose,
Sometimes he is very runny
But he is never funny.

My best friend is chocolate.

Michael McCormick (11)
Tayport Primary School

I Went Into Town One Day

I went into town one day
I saw my uncle Jim,
I went up to say, 'Hello'
But he was looking rather dim.
He put his hand in his pocket
And took out a £10 note.
He put it in my hand
And said, 'Go and buy a brand new coat.'

I went into some shops with him.
He showed me what he had bought,
I told him they were very nice,
But that's not what I really thought
I said I had to go now
Because I was getting rather bored.
He said, 'OK
But mind your head
And don't walk into that door!'

Fiona Dempster (11)
Tayport Primary School

Mission To Mars

Mission to Mars,
Mission to Mars,
It would be fun visiting Mars
In a spaceship visiting Mars.
Beep, bop, beep, bop.
In a spaceship visiting Mars.
Beep, bop, beep, bop,
In a spaceship visiting Mars.
Black Rock,
Blue Rock,
Even in Blackpool there's rock.
Red rock,
Blue rock,
But that's why Mars is called the Red Planet.
It would be fun visiting Mars,
That's why it's called mission to Mars.

Stewart Adamson (11)
Tayport Primary School

The Bee

Buzz, buzz, buzzing bee,
Busy making honey in the tree
Looks delicious, smells delicious
And it's going to end up on my plate for tea!

Steven Soutar (11)
Tayport Primary School

My Brother

My brother is annoying,
He drives me up the wall.
But sometimes he is cute,
Because he is so small.

He's always on his skateboard,
Even in the dark.
And then he falls and bumps his head
On the ramps at the park.

We are sometimes naughty
And fight with each other,
But I think on the whole:
I still love my brother.

Charlotte Sloan (11)
Tayport Primary School

Dinosaurs

Dinosaurs are really neat
Especially with their giant feet,
They stomp around all day and night
And give us humans a real good fright.

Some eat plants, some eat meat,
I hope they don't eat Uncle Pete.
But best of all to this day,
The dinosaurs have passed away.

John Ricketts (11)
Tayport Primary School

Birdies

Birdy, birdy fly
Round and round the house all day
Look, he flew away.

Jordan Taylor (11)
Tayport Primary School

Star

I saw a star in the night sky,
It's brighter than the sun,
It shone into the window
And rose back into the sky.
In the morning I saw it again,
It would not go away,
But after breakfast when I came back,
I saw the star was gone.
I looked around and never saw a thing,
I'm sure I will see it shine tonight again.

Jane Solonitsyna (11)
Tayport Primary School

Super Fish

It whizzes past
It's really fast,
It's Super Fish.

It sings its song,
It makes a pong,
It's Super Fish.

It's really thin,
It eats out of a tin,
It's Super Fish.

Super Fish,
It's really cool,
Super Fish
Lives in a swimming pool.

Super Fish,
It's really neat,
Super Fish,
It likes to eat.

Hugh von Arnim (11)
Tayport Primary School

The Moon

The moon was bright,
On the night,
I looked at it with glee,
But as I looked,
I saw it staring back at me.
It was smiling,
So I did too,
But when I started to do kung fu
It went away.
The next night
I stared at it again,
Trying hard to find it
With my friend,
But after a while it turned up,
Bright yellow like a buttercup,
So then again I smiled
And looked up with glee,
Then I started laughing,
But the moon just copied me!
So from then on,
Every night I looked,
The moon shone,
Until one night I forgot,
And never looked at it again!

Arwen Ogilvy (11)
Tayport Primary School